felt

felt

Designs by
India Flint and
Toyoko Sugiwaka

MURDOCH BOOKS

contents

techniques

projects

Introduction

Felt is the simple and magical outcome when wool, moisture and friction are combined. It is probably the oldest known textile, perhaps discovered by accident after the first wolf crept in to join the humans sheltering in caves and began shedding hair. In a world without vacuum cleaners, the fluffy hairs underfoot would build up, forming drifts here and there. As these were soft and comfortable, our ancestors may have collected them to make their sleeping quarters more cosy, and then marvelled that warmth, moisture and friction could transform fluff into firm, useful fabric.

It is possible that early humans then began to gather the soft undercoats of animals, caught on twigs and bushes, from which to produce this useful textile. The original wild sheep known to early humans had strong guard hairs, with softer fur underneath, a little like that of a Border collie or German shepherd dog. Domestication of sheep and selective breeding for softer wool have produced the range of fleeces we know today.

antarctic hat variation With fleece curls inside and a wing decoration on top (see page 39).

There are many stories about the possible origins of felt. One has it that one of King Solomon's sons, observing the woollen coats enjoyed by sheep, cut the wool from one of his flock, and then tried and tried in vain to fashion himself a coat from it. Finally, in a rage, he urinated on it and jumped on it, finding to his amazement that a firm cloth was formed. Urine was still used in nineteenth-century Britain as an assistant in the fulling (shrinking and firming) of cloth, as well as an important mordant in dyeing and a 'wool conditioner'.

There are very few old felt remnants left, the reason being that felt is a utility fabric, and was most likely in use until worn out. When something of substance did remain, the old became the base for making the new. Also, wool is easily composted and breaks down if returned to the environment (many farmers use waste wool as an excellent slow-release fertilizer, rich in nitrogen, to mulch young trees).

The Pazyryk felts (housed in the Hermitage Museum in St Petersburg, Russia) are the oldest known remnants, dated to between 600 and 200 BC, and were preserved under exceptional circumstances in regions of permafrost in the Altai region of Siberia. They were dyed blue, red and yellow using plant dyes, and the colours remain vibrant to this day. The Ürümqi mummies found late last century in Central Asia also wore items made of felt.

Wool felt is still used today to make boots (*valenki*) in Russia, houses (yurts and gers) and for buffering the dampers on pianos. It is used for carpets, bags, filters, for protecting ice hockey players, as saddle packing and for making soft, warm coats and hats, ideal for European winters. In recent years, felt has enjoyed a revival, as fashion designers have discovered the amazing properties of this versatile cloth, warm and non-fraying, which can be moulded to the human body, used thickly or lightly, draped or crisply formed. Felt can be made by hand in spaces as small as a table top, or commercially produced in huge factories. It is a simple and yet deeply satisfying craft.

About felt

Anyone who has accidentally included a favourite fine merino jumper in a hot machine wash will know only too well that the process of felt making is ongoing and irreversible. The strength of felt lies in the structure of the wool itself. A single filament of wool is actually stronger than a thread of steel of the same diameter. It has small scales on the surface, just as human hair does. When wool fibre is wetted, the scales lift and the fibre swells. If there is friction, the fibres creep closer together. As the fibres become dry again, the scales flatten, locking on to any fibres that may be crossing them.

The more wool fibres are agitated, the faster they creep closer together. Once they are dried, their grip on each other is very strong and will not be loosened until the cloth is moistened again. (Dreadlocks are constructed using a felting process.) This is why felt must be dried in the desired shape, and why woollen clothing should be dried on a support without the use of pegs (otherwise the marks will show until the next soaking).

Wool is a miraculous material, highly elastic and also fire resistant, and able to hold up to 25 per cent of its dry weight in moisture before it begins to feel damp. It is a protein fibre, is chemically neutral and can be dyed using many plant varieties as well as chemical dyes (including synthetically coloured foodstuffs such as drink concentrates and jelly powder). Wool can also be used to bond with other fibres, including silk, cotton, flax, hemp, ramie and soy silk, in the felting process.

Yurts

Traditional yurts (known in Mongolia as gers) are domed tents that have been used by nomadic Mongolian people for thousands of years. Easy to assemble, dismantle and transport, they are also very sturdy, and able to withstand storms. Three-quarters of Mongolians still live in yurts, many of them in permanent yurt settlements.

Yurts are constructed of poles covered with a thick layer of felt (and sometimes reinforced with canvas). The thickness of the felt can be adjusted to suit the temperature, and the bottom of the felt can be rolled up for ventilation. At the centre of the dome is a hole for ventilation and light.

Washing wool

Contrary to popular belief, wool can actually be washed in hot water. The trick is not to vary the temperature of the water by more than 5°C (9°F) between successive baths or to agitate the wool. Once extremes of temperature and agitation or friction are introduced, felting is inevitable.

Pleating and folding felt

Felt has a 'memory' for the shape in which it dries, so you can introduce pleats, folds and wrinkles if you want. Clothes pegs can be used to hold the folds while the felt dries, but keep in mind that the peg will leave an imprint. Alternatively, hold the pleats or folds in place with tacking stitches, unpicking them once the felt is dry.

special effects Leicester Longwool gives texture to the Shaggy rug with fleece curls (page 40).

What fibres can be felted?

Only wool makes true felt, as the structure of the felt depends upon the scaly structure of the wool fibres. Only sheep produce wool. Other fibre-producing animals include (but are not limited to) goats, alpacas, camels, rabbits, cats and dogs — all of which produce hair, not wool. Their product varies in usefulness; for example, the long, soft winter coat shed by horses and ponies in the springtime will not felt at all (even when blended with wool). Rabbit fur is the foundation of many felt hats, but is bonded using a highly toxic glue for durability. Industrial felt is usually made of synthetic waste products, bonded using a flat-bed needle-felting technique.

Various breeds of sheep produce wool suitable for felting, with different breeds giving different effects. Wool is classified as fine, medium or strong according to its thickness (usually expressed in microns; see page 9). The Australian Merino is the optimum breed for clothing felt, as it produces the finest wool (a British breed of sheep with strong wool could have a micron count up to twice that of a Merino). Merino wool is available throughout the U.K., Europe, Asia and North America.

In northern Europe, Friesian and Gotland sheep are popular for felting. In middle Europe, the Austrian Bergschaf is much used. In New Zealand, the locally bred Perendale is good for durable, sturdy felt. Stronger wools from breeds such as Leicester Longwool, Romney and Border Leicester are suitable for floor rugs. Merino crosses of these breeds will often produce good-quality, easy-felting wool.

In Mongolia, sheep's wool is principally used for yurts and gers, but also for rugs. Mongolian wool is available in Europe from felting suppliers.

Fibres other than wool can be used to decorate wool felt by either blending them with the sliver (the scoured, combed and carded wool fibres ready for felting) or simply laying them on the surface prior to felting. Silk, flax, hemp, ingeo (corn silk), alpaca and soy silk are all available in sliver form. Angora (rabbit fur), cotton fluff and mohair (from Angora goats) can also be incorporated into felt. Woven textiles will bond with wool, provided there are air spaces in the weave. A good test is to try to breathe through the textile; if breath passes easily through the cloth, wool fibres are likely to do so as well. Lovely effects can be achieved by felting onto patterned cloth.

Terms used in felting

Carding Wool is processed between two drums covered in small metal spikes to remove vegetable matter, soil and knots. Carded batting (which can also be produced on a small scale using a hand-operated drum carder) is a useful base for felting.

Combing After carding, wool is combed so that all the fibres lie in the same direction.

Crimp This refers to the natural waviness of the wool. The degree of crimp varies with the breed and the thickness of the wool.

Fleece wool Technically (in industry terms), fleece wool is the highest quality of the wool shorn from the sheep (generally wool from the side of the body).

Fulling This refers to the process of shrinking, firming and finishing soft felt (see page 10) so that it becomes dense and durable. This is generally done by rolling, but can also be achieved through dropping, kneading and beating.

Hard (or 'finished') felt Felt that has been fulled so that it no longer decreases visibly in size when rolled (however, vigorous machine washing can still shrink finished felt). It will feel firm to the touch and will be impossible to pull apart.

Lustre The brilliant glossy appearance of wool from British longwool breeds.

Microns The micron is the international unit of wool measurement. Although a micron is a mere one-millionth of a metre, experienced wool classers can usually make quite accurate estimates (to within 1–2 microns, particularly with regard to Merino wool). Wool of low micron count is generally referred to as being 'fine', whereas that of a high micron count is called 'strong' and requires considerable effort to felt. Merino wool comes in a range of 17–28 microns (the latter would be considered rather coarse, the former much in demand by Italian suit makers). Leicester Longwool

Equipment

Felting requires little specialized equipment. Most projects can be made using the following: soap; bubble wrap, for making templates and rolling up the item to be felted; a plastic non-slip mat or plastic fly-wire, useful as an intermediary or protective layer when rubbing soft, wet felt (fly-wire is particularly useful when bonding additional soft felts to the main body of felt using a scrunched piece of plastic or the wooden felting tool, shown above, to work the surface); a sushi mat and large bamboo blind, for rolling small and large items respectively; a watering can and hand-mister; and nylon cloth, for rolling up delicate felts at the beginning of the fulling stage after removing the felt from the mat or bubble wrap.

You may find it useful to buy wool carders (shown at the right of the photograph); these consist of two flat brushes studded with pins, between which fleece is stroked to straighten and separate the fibres. At the left of the photo is an improvised smoothing implement made from a cement-working tool with ribbed vinyl sheeting stapled over it; this is used to encourage fluffy parts to bond together or to add small pieces of pre-felt if repairing thin areas or adding decoration.

fulling This refers to the shrinking and hardening of felt, achieved through rolling or massage.

pre-felts These semi-felted pieces can be joined to each other, or to a background fabric.

Hint

You can make quite large felted pieces in a small workspace, by using a sushi mat to make small pre-felts then joining them together; this is the method used for the Patchwork blanket (page 62).

Caring for felt

Because feltmaking is a continuous and irreversible process, any vigorous washing will shrink the felt. Big felt pieces are best laid on a mesh support or rolled in a bath, and gently hosed or sprayed. Small felt pieces should be very gently handwashed, making sure the temperature of the water is kept within a 5°C (9°F) range (see also page 7). Felt can be ironed while slightly damp, using a hot iron if desired. The important thing is always to dry the felt in the required shape, as it has a 'memory'. If folding felt for storage, acid-free tissue paper helps to prevent creasing, and good-quality moth repellent is essential.

To keep insects away, regular airing is important. Camphor-wood chips and boxes are both very good, and cedar balls also work quite well. Lavender, however, actually attracts moths due to its fragrance.

has a range of about 32–40 (in adult sheep), with rams generally having quite strong wool. Lincoln sheep are the strongest (British) longwool breed, with micron counts in the high 40s and low 50s. Their wool, which resembles curly human hair, is in demand for dolls' wigs, and was used to make human wigs in the past.

Pre-felt When the wool fibres have bonded sufficiently that the felt (when dry) holds together when lifted, but is still fluffy, the piece is called a pre-felt.

Raw fleece This describes unwashed (or unscoured) and untreated wool as shorn from the sheep. Raw wool contains vegetable matter picked up while the animal is grazing, natural secretions such as lanolin, and various other substances.

Roving See sliver.

Scouring Scouring is the process of washing the wool to remove the lanolin and dirt. After scouring, the wool is dried before being carded.

Sliver This refers to wool that has been scoured (washed), carded and combed, and formed into a thick, soft, straight (that is, untwisted) rope. This is how the wool is prepared for spinning into yarn. Felters find sliver most useful for making felt of an even thickness. In Britain, sliver is known as roving.

Soft felt At soft-felt stage, the work may be lifted and turned even though it is wet, and will not pull apart with the weight of the water. However, it still feels quite soft and can be easily stretched.

Staple The length of the wool fibre. Merino has a staple of 10–12.5 cm (4–5 inches); this is the growth for one year. Leicester Longwool can be up to 27 cm (11 inches).

Superwash wool This denotes wool with fibres that have been treated with silicon to ensure they don't felt while being washed; it is therefore totally unsuited to felting.

raw fleece Sheep produce fleece in various shades of cream, grey, brown and black.

sliver Sliver is cleaned, combed and carded wool that is ready to be spun or felted.

Making felt

To begin understanding felt, simply take a handful of wool fleece, wet it with hot, soapy water, and roll it around vigorously between the palms of your hands. In a very short space of time, the fluffy fleece will transform into a tight, firm woollen ball and you will have made felt.

Flat felt

The next step is to make flat felt. A simple and cheap piece of equipment for this is a sushi mat, which can be used on the kitchen sink. You can use raw fleece for the felting, or purchase wool sliver, which is more pleasant to use and has been scoured, carded and combed so that the wool is clean and the fibres are aligned.

1 Unroll the sushi mat. Gently pull tufts of wool from the end of the sliver and lay them on the mat so that they are all facing the same way, with each row slightly overlapping the previous one.

2 Lay out another layer, with the fibres at right angles to the first layer. Sprinkle the wool with warm, slightly soapy water (too much soap will create bubbles, which will decrease contact between the fibres).

3 Lifting the edge of the mat slightly, gently roll up the mat with the wool inside.

Using wetting agents

While it isn't essential to use a wetting agent when making felt, it does speed up the process. One or two drops of eco-friendly detergent to a 10-litre (2-gallon) bucket is enough to begin with. Then, as you work more with the piece, you'll find soap very useful, both to stick down any loose ends and hold them in place as you work, and as a lubricant so the felt doesn't catch on your fingers. While many people believe that the alkalinity of the soap promotes the felting, it has probably more to do with its lubricating and wetting qualities. If the fibres are well wetted, the little scales on the wool swell and lift up. As the felt is rolled, the individual fibres slide ever closer together. This is why felt appears to 'shrink' in the direction of the rolling action. When the finished felt has been rinsed and dried, the scales on the wool will have flattened again, and will have 'locked down' over any fibres that happen to be crossing them. This is what makes felt so strong, and why feltmaking is an irreversible and continuous process.

step one Pull wool from the end of the bundle of sliver and lay it on a bamboo mat.

step two Lay down the second layer of sliver, with the fibres running at right angles to the first.

step two continued Sprinkle the wool with warm, slightly soapy water.

Alternative method

Another felting technique, used for several of the smaller projects in this book, is to grasp and squeeze the felted item a number of times, first horizontally then vertically, rather than rolling it. Doing this in hot water then in cold hastens the felting process.

dampened sliver Once damp, the sliver will regain its natural wave as the fibres 'relax'.

Put a large rubber band over each end of the finished roll to keep it together. Then roll the bundle back and forth over the ridged draining surface of the kitchen sink. After 30 rolls, remove the rubber bands and unroll carefully. Use the mat to stretch the felt if any small wrinkles have formed. Re-roll the mat from the other end, re-apply the rubber bands and roll again 30 times. Undo the bundle again; the wool should now be sufficiently bonded that it can be picked up as one piece. The felt, though unfinished, is at a stage at which it may be handled. This is known as a 'pre-felt'. It is still quite soft, and may be bonded to other pre-felts.

4 Firm the edges of the felt by folding them inwards slightly and patting them with lightly soaped fingers. Alternatively, leave the edges flat and firm them by gentle 'massage', running soapy fingers over the surface in a light circular motion (initially using the sort of pressure one would use to apply cream to the face).

5 To finish the felt, keep rolling it from different directions until it is quite firm, adding more soapy water if required. This is called 'fulling' the felt. You will notice that the felt 'shrinks' in the direction of rolling. This is because the scales on the wool fibres allow them to travel in only one direction, so they must creep closer together as friction is applied. It is important to have wool fibres laid out crossing each other for the strength of the felt, and also to roll the felt in both directions to ensure proper bonding of the fibres. The finished piece of felt will only measure two-thirds of the size originally laid out. This is because the fibres have all moved closer together during the felting process.

step three Roll up the wool in the mat, lifting it a little to allow air to escape.

step three continued Roll the bundle back and forth the required number of times.

step four Use lightly soaped fingers to firm the edge of the felt.

Tips for felting

Using a washing machine

A front-loading washing machine is a wonderful felting tool. The fast-wash cycle can be used to rapidly finish felt where control of size is not critical — the felt will be very tough. This method is especially useful for making felt balls and sturdy bathmats. Wool- or hand-wash cycles are ideal for controlled finish of felt, repeating as necessary. Remember that machine-fulled felt tends to be somewhat fluffier than mat-rolled felt. Top-loading machines may be used to extract water by spinning, but are not helpful for felting flat pieces as the central agitator tends to rip the felt. However, small objects such as balls, bags and slippers may be fulled in a top loader. Protect them in a net washing bag and include them with a load of clothes (for additional friction).

Rolling

You may find that to finish your felt, you need to do more rolling than that suggested in the instructions. This is because there are many factors that can affect felting, including the strength (thickness) and breed of the wool, the temperature of the room or water and the pressure you exert on the work as you are rolling it. Even the quality of the water can make a difference; wool felts more rapidly when the water is alkaline. On the other hand, a heavy salt content will affect the behaviour of the soap or wetting agent. Experience will enable you to gauge more easily just how much effort will be required.

Try using a thick dowel or length of plastic down-pipe in the centre of your roll, whether using a bamboo mat or blind, or bubble wrap. This can make for more even felting, as sometimes when a felt is tightly rolled, the middle of the roll can felt more firmly than the outer edge.

Hints for making thick and thin felts

When making thick felts, wet each layer as you build up the wool layers.

Very fine felts can be strengthened by adding a layer of butter muslin (cheesecloth) between fine layers of sliver. This technique is sometimes referred to as 'nuno' felt ('nuno' being the Japanese word for cloth). The cloth may (but does not have to) be hemmed first. If you wish, lay extra sliver at the edges and fold the cloth over so that it creates a felted hem.

Using bubble wrap

Bubble wrap has various applications for felting. It is often used for making templates, and can also be employed to pick up a soft, wet, fragile piece of felt so that it can be turned (above); reverse-roll it by laying the wrap over the top of the piece, then pick up and roll the felt and bubble wrap together.

Bubble wrap can be used to make large areas of pre-felt quite rapidly. When used to roll felt, it has the advantage over using a bamboo mat in that the felt is easier to peel away from the plastic and that any applied moisture is retained in the roll. Also, bubble wrap is easily dried and stored away if space is short. The disadvantage is that one needs to be very careful about pressing air bubbles out of the wetted wool before rolling up the wrap, as there is no way for them to escape (unlike in the bamboo mat, where air can escape through the space between the slats). While bubble wrap is good for making garments, scarves and small items, thick rugs are still best made in bamboo mats or blinds in the traditional manner.

Plant dyes

All plants give some sort of colour in the dye pot, some more exciting than others. Avoid using protected or slow-growing plants and anything you can't identify.

Commonly available plant materials such as onion skins give delightful colours. Many weeds (such as *Hypericum perforatum*, or St John's wort, a weed of wastelands such as railway sidings and roadsides, and *Oxalis pes-caprae*, or soursob) are useful dye plants.

Eucalypts and acacias give colour, too. Leaves from the former can give colours ranging from green through gold to red and brown; leaves, seedpods and bark from acacia yield lovely golds and browns as well.

The scent of a plant is often a clue to colour; highly aromatic leaves contain acids and oils which either are dyes or will assist in the dye process. Eucalypts are a good example. Also, if colour can be rubbed from the leaf, it may (but does not always) indicate dye potential.

naturally dyed sliver All these bundles of sliver have been dyed using plant extracts.

Colour and decoration

Colouring your work

Sliver is available ready dyed in a range of colours. If you want to dye your own, you will need natural or synthetic dyes, and a traditional dye pot if using the stovetop, or a plastic container in a microwave oven. Brightly coloured drink concentrates often make excellent wool dyes. It is vital to heat and cool the sliver slowly, and not to stir it while it is being heated (or it will begin to felt).

If using plant extracts, make the extract first, then gently lower the dry sliver into the dye bath and heat for 30–60 minutes, keeping the temperature just below a simmer so that the surface of the dye bath is steaming slightly but not moving. Allow the sliver to cool in the solution, then place in a stainless steel, plastic or enamel strainer over a bucket to drain, and gently press out excess moisture. Dry in the shade. So long as toxic adjunct mordants (see below) are not used there will be no need to rinse, as this will occur during felting. If using synthetic dyes, adhere to the manufacturer's instructions for dye preparation, remembering not to stir the sliver. *It is most important never to dye anything in a pot that you use for cooking food, as the dyestuffs, whether natural or synthetic, may be toxic.*

A note on mordants

A mordant is a substance used to fix or alter colours obtained from dyes. Toxic adjunct mordants are the traditional metallic salt mordants such as chrome (potassium bichromate), tin (stannous chloride), copper (copper sulphate) and iron (ferrous sulphate). All are poisons and should not be used; they are dangerous in powdered form and difficult to dispose of responsibly in the spent solution. However, using pots made of these metals as the dye vessel can influence the colour of the dyebath. In general (but not always), iron shifts many dyes to purples and blacks; copper enhances greens; brass enhances greens and yellows, depending on the dye-plant that you are using; aluminium tends to enrich colours. Stainless steel is non-reactive. Otherwise, stick to mordants that you might find in and around the kitchen. Plant dyes for wool work best in an acidic environment (pH 7 or less). Vinegar will help lower the pH and also acts as a wool conditioner. Alum (potassium aluminium sulphate) is a traditional mordant for wool; use it sparingly, because it is an alkali and can make the wool quite 'sticky' to handle.

Decorating the surface

You may like to experiment with decorative effects for the surface of your felt. Remember that the design is more likely to stay where you've placed it if you work in reverse, that is, by building up layers from the front. You can make spots, stripes, flowers or various other abstract, geometric or figurative designs.

Sushi felt

Another way of making a pattern is to use the sushi felt technique (as shown in the photographs below). This produces spots with a swirly, spiral effect.

Begin by laying out sliver as though making a sushi roll; first lay down a wide strip of sliver in one colour, then add successive layers in other colours along one edge, each narrower than the last. All layers should be roughly the same length (there is no need to be exact; they will be trimmed later). Misting lightly with a water spray can help to keep the layers together.

Roll up the bundle carefully from one long side. Using sharp scissors, cut the log into slices about 1 cm (⅜ in) thick and arrange them decoratively on the bamboo mat or bubble wrap.

Cover the sushi decorations with two layers of sliver at right angles to each other, then dampen and felt in the usual manner.

decorations Crisp-edged spots can be formed on a bamboo mat.

adding texture Add texture to the decorations by forming holes with the fingers.

sushi felt Lay out sliver as though making a sushi roll, in successively narrower strips.

sushi felt, step two Roll up the sliver from one long side, then cut into slices.

sushi felt, step three Lay the sushi pieces onto the bamboo mat, then cover with sliver.

Taking care of your body

Make sure your felting table is at the correct height in relation to your body, so that no damage occurs to your back. A good height is 5–10 cm (2–4 in) below your navel when you are laying out wool. If you can sit on a stool that allows you to keep your back straight while you are rolling the felt, so much the better.

Have frequent breaks during long layouts and rolling sessions, stretching your arms, legs and back, rolling your shoulders and making sure that no areas of tension build up. Remember that wool can hold a great deal of water; for that reason, avoid trying to pick up large wet rugs.

Spots

For spotted felt, roll a small amount of sliver between the palms of your hands to make loose fluffy balls. Lay these on the felting mat and build up the layers as required. For rainbow spots, make sushi felt (see page 15).

Stripes

Cut sliver into lengths, and then split it. These stripes will be wavy after the felting process, once the wetted wool relaxes and regains its natural curl. For more precise stripes, make a pre-felt and cut it into strips. For a tartan effect, combine stripes as above with lengths of wool yarn to build up the desired pattern.

Blending colours

Take handfuls of sliver in the colours you wish to mix. Hold them one over the other and gently pull apart. Repeat until the colours are blended satisfactorily.

Adding texture

Wool's wonderful bonding qualities can be used to make richly textured decorative surfaces. Try felting natural fibres such as silk, flax and hemp (all available in sliver form) in fine layers on the surface. Soy silk, cotton waste and silk off-cuts left over from overlocking can also be used to add interest to your work.

stripes Make stripes by alternating pieces of sliver in two or more colours.

wavy lines Wetted wool relaxes and its natural wave returns, forming wavy lines in the sliver.

grid pattern For straight edges, cut pre-felts into the desired shape, then lay them flat or interlaced.

Tails, tassels and handles

Sliver can be made into ropes, for example as a tail or the handle on a bag. Take a section of sliver. If you intend sewing both ends to the item, felt the whole piece between your palms or on a mat. Or felt only the middle section or one end; the unfelted end(s) can then be felted onto the body of the item for a seamless join.

Making a flower

Quite delicate flowers can be made as part of a pattern on the surface of your felt, as shown in the three photographs below.

Take a short section of coloured sliver, then roll it up spiral-fashion with your fingers to make a flat circle. Lay this down on the bubble wrap or bamboo mat to form the centre of the flower.

To make petals with rounded ends, take a short section of sliver, lightly dampen each end, fold the sliver in half and twist the two ends together. Alternatively, to make petals with pointed ends, twist both ends of the folded piece of sliver, then fold up the wispy tail at the bottom to give a neat finish. Place the petals on top of the flower centre, then lay down sliver to form the background of the piece. Then begin felting as normal. To stop the flower pattern from moving about as you felt it, you can lay a piece of plastic fly-wire atop the design. Then begin felting through the fly-wire by rubbing with a scrunched-up plastic shopping bag.

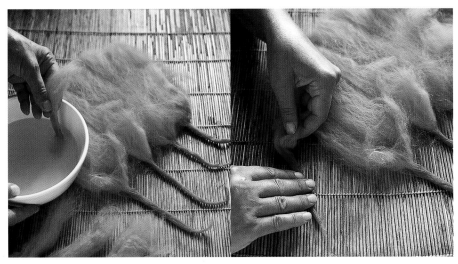

to make a tail, step one Wet sections of sliver with warm soapy water.

tail, step two Felt one end. The other end is then felted to the item (such as the cat toys on page 79).

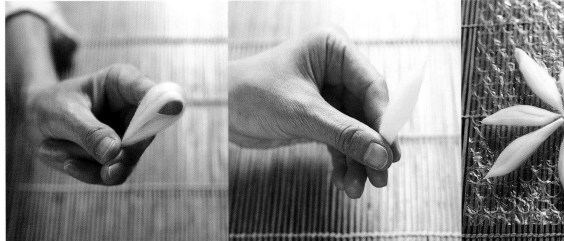

petals, step one For rounded petals, fold the sliver in half and twist both ends together.

petals, step two Felt the folded end of the piece of sliver to create pointy petals.

flower Put a coloured centre down on the bubble wrap, then arrange the petals on top.

Beads

Making beads from felt is a simple and delightful amusement, and one of the best ways for beginner feltmakers to understand the process of making felt. Two techniques are described here: round beads, made from a ball of sliver; and sushi beads, constructed from layers of sliver that are rolled up, felted then sliced.

Felted beads can be used as buttons, strung together to make necklaces, suspended as a mobile over a baby's cot, beaded to decorate hatpins, or even given to a spoiled pet to play with.

Materials
Wool sliver

Wool yarn or other threads, for embellishment
(optional)

Washed fleece or rag, for forming larger balls
(optional)

Linen thread, pearl embroidery cotton
or good-quality machine-sewing thread
(use 6 strands together), for stringing
beads (optional)

Tools
Soap

Bubble wrap

Hand-mister

Craft knife, sharp knife or razor blade
(if making sushi beads)

Sharp or crewel needle, for stringing beads
(optional)

Size
Each bead approximately 2.5 cm (1 in)
in diameter

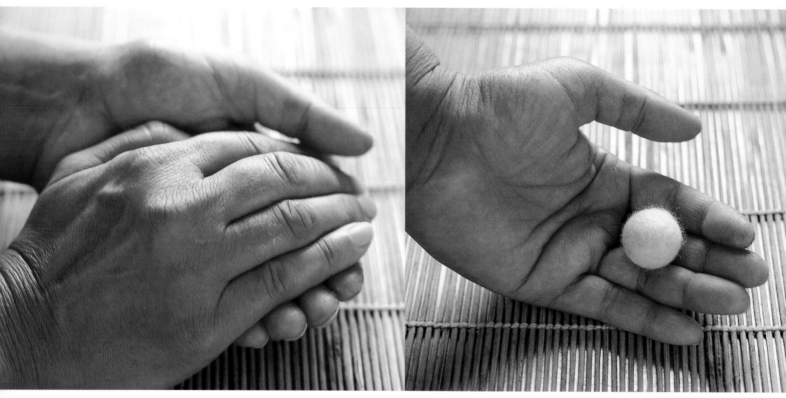

round beads, step one After wetting the ball of fluff, roll it gently between your palms, gradually applying more pressure as the felt becomes firmer.

the finished round bead After wetting and rolling, the finished felted bead will be substantially smaller and harder than the ball of fluff you started with.

Hint

For beads of uniform size, cut the sliver into uniform lengths, and take equal amounts for each bead. For extra accuracy, weigh sliver on jewellers' scales (it is very light) after making the first sample (weigh the sample when completely dry). Also, pressure, moisture and heat of the felting process will all make a difference to the size of the bead. If you keep the variables relatively constant and use similar amounts of wool each time, there won't be discernible differences.

Round beads

1 To make a small felt ball, cut wool sliver into 3 cm (1¼ in) lengths, tease it out with your fingers, dampen it with warm soapy water and roll it between the palms of the hands until felted, about 10 minutes. Go softly at first, until you feel the felt begin to harden a little, then apply more pressure.

If you want to add interest to the surface, wind small strips of sliver around the bead before it is fully felted, soap the surface well and continue felting. You can also stitch on to the partly felted bead using wool yarn or other threads.

2 To make a bigger bead or a small ball, take a handful of washed fleece (or even a scrap of rag), scrunch it into a ball shape and wrap a length of spare yarn around it to keep the shape together. Then wind small strips of sliver around the outside, building them up until the core is well covered.

3 Moisten the whole with warm soapy water, and soap the outside a little as well so that it doesn't stick to your hands. Finish the felt by rolling it between your hands, on a piece of bubble wrap, or on the draining ridges of the kitchen sink. Rinse well and allow to dry. When completely dry, use as desired.

variation: hatpin Use a large darning needle as a hatpin; for decoration, add a wooden bead and a felt bead, and tie ribbon or thread to the eye of the needle.

sushi beads Layers of sliver are rolled into a log, felted then cut into slices. String them together from side to side, not top to bottom, to best show their colours.

Sushi beads

Lay out a fine layer of sliver, about 30 cm (12 in) square. Place another fine layer in a different colour on top, at right angles to the first. Do this a few more times, then take a couple of narrow strips of sliver, also 30 cm (12 in) long, and lay them along the edge at one long side of the pile (see the photographs on page 15). Mist the wool with a hand-mister. Roll up the bundle from one long side, with the narrow strips of sliver forming the core of the roll. By gently rolling the bundle away from you along the work surface, it will tighten on itself. After a while, you will be able to dampen it more,

and felt more vigorously. When it is strong enough, toss it into the washing machine for a final beating. This helps to make the beads very strong. When fully felted, allow to dry. When completely dry, slice the sushi roll using a sharp knife, craft knife or razor blade (scissors will squash the felt). String the beads from side to side, rather than top to bottom, so that their delightful colours can be appreciated.

Making bobbles

To make weighted bobbles that can be used to keep the flap of a bag down, without the need for loops or holes, wrap the wool sliver around a small river pebble and felt as described at left.

As a variation, use different coloured layers and slice the finished felt open at the end, taking out the pebble. The striped sculptural shape can also be attached to a pin for an unusual brooch.

Bowls on a ball

From time to time (for example, if you have made the Patchwork blanket on page 62), you may find yourself with an abundance of pre-felts. These are always useful for decoration, but can also be used to make quick and delightful gifts such as bowls. This simple project uses a ball as a template to give a symmetrical shape, but this technique can also be used on irregularly shaped objects for a less symmetrical look.

If you use a different colour of sliver for each layer, the result will be an interesting striped edge to the finished bowl.

Materials
Pre-felts
Wool yarn or other threads
Beads or buttons, for embellishment (optional)

Tools
Plastic ball
Darning needle
Scissors
Soap
Bubble wrap (optional)

materials You will need a plastic ball, some pre-felts and wool yarn or other thread to sew the pre-felts in layers around the ball.

step one Wrap the pre-felt quite tightly around the ball until the ball is completely covered. Here, the pre-felt has been made in the form of strips.

Shaping pre-felts The height of the pre-felt pieces should equal roughly half the circumference of the ball. Their width should be roughly half their height.

1 Find a plastic ball (about the size of a basketball is good, but you can use smaller ones as well). Take pieces of pre-felt and layer them on to the ball. You may need to taper them at each end (see left) so that wrinkles are avoided, but make sure they overlap. Join them with stitches using wool (this will felt), silk or cotton (these won't shrink, so may bubble up decoratively) and a large darning needle, making sure you don't pierce the ball. Have at least four layers over the whole ball, making sure that the last layer is quite firmly stitched around the ball. It should be fairly tight, as the wool will initially sag when wetted.

2 Once the ball is prepared, it can be a great bath-time amusement to pat the wet ball firmly (while sitting in the warm bath) until the felt is firm. Alternatively, wrap it in bubble wrap and roll it around on the draining ridges of the kitchen sink or, best of all, put it into a short-wash cycle in a front-loading washing machine, along with items such as jeans that won't stick easily to the felt. This is also a good way to make several bowls at once. If using the washing machine, begin the process by hand-felting until the wool stops sagging.

3 When the wool is fully felted around the ball, mark the circumference of the ball

step one continued Stitch through the layers of pre-felt around the ball, using wool or other yarn and a darning needle. Stitch the last layer particularly tightly.

step two Wet well, then felt by hand, or wrap in bubble wrap and roll it around on the draining ridges of a sink. Finish it in the washing machine for a very firm surface.

with a piece of yarn and carefully make an incision in the felt, so that you can slide the lower point of your scissors under the felt, making sure not to cut the ball. Cut right around the ball, until your two bowls are revealed. The edges will be striped from the different coloured layers you have built up.

Variations

For smaller bowls, wrap sliver around the ball, and then wrap woollen yarn over the sliver, securing firmly. Wet, soap and rub the ball around between your palms. When the yarn has bonded with the sliver, toss

the ball into the washing machine to finish felting. (Don't use a tennis ball, as the felt will bond with the ball.) Cut open carefully.

Add a pattern by carefully snipping small leaf shapes into the top layer or two of the finished surface with a small, very sharp pair of scissors; the different colours of wool from the layers of pre-felts will give an attractive effect.

You can stitch beads or buttons onto the bowls and use them for displaying Easter eggs, buttons, nuts or river pebbles.

Hint

Sometimes the felt-covered balls are simply too beautiful to cut into bowls. In this case, leave them covered in felt for an unusual cushion, or as a house-toy. Felted balls tend not to roll as far as plain plastic ones, nor do they bounce.

Stone door prop

step one Roll up the stone in the square of pre-felt, easing and adjusting the pre-felt to ensure the stone is well covered.

step three Wet the stone in hot soapy water then rub it with your hands or roll it about on a piece of bubble wrap until well felted.

This variation on the bowl-on-a-ball technique produces a useful door prop with a rustic appeal.

Materials

Wool sliver to make pre-felt

A smooth river or beach stone
  about the size of a brick
  (or use a house brick)

Wool yarn

Tools

Large darning needle

Bucket

Soap

Towel

Bubble wrap

1 Make a piece of pre-felt, about 60 cm (24 in) square, using four layers of wool. If you wish to incorporate patterning, do it on the part of the square that will be on the outside of the bundle. Lay the pre-felt pattern side down. Put the stone on the pre-felt and roll it up, easing and adjusting the pre-felt so the stone is well covered.

2 Secure the pre-felt with some stitches, using wool yarn and a large darning needle (as for the Bowl on a ball, page 24). The stitches can become a decorative feature.

3 Dip the woolly stone into a bucket of hot soapy water, and begin to rub it gently with your hands. Keep working your way around the stone, becoming more vigorous as the felt begins to firm. You may find that rolling the stone around on a pad made of a folded towel, covered by a piece of bubble wrap (bubble side up), is helpful.

4 Continue rubbing and rolling the stone on the bubble wrap until the felt is firm. Rinse, then allow to dry. The felt-covered stone prop will be much quieter than a bare one.

Simple pod bag

This organic-looking round bag, constructed around a simple donut-shaped bubble-wrap template, is easy to make. The handle can be left plain, as in the photograph at right, or wrapped, as in the examples on the following pages.

Adjust the size of the template to produce a bigger or smaller bag, making the template about 50 per cent larger all round than you want the finished bag to be.

This technique can also be used to make a beret (see page 31). For a small beret, cut a bubble-wrap template 30 cm (12 in) in diameter; for medium, it will need to be 35 cm (14 in); and for large, 40 cm (16 in).

Materials
Wool sliver
Pre-felt, for reinforcement
Wool yarn or other thread, if making wrapped
  handle
Petersham ribbon, if making the beret variation
  (optional)

Tools
Bubble wrap, for template
Darning needle, if making wrapped handle
Soap
Bubble wrap or bamboo mat

Size
Approximately 28 cm (11 in) in diameter

step two Once you have laid out the layers of sliver, put the template on top, then the donut-shaped piece of pre-felt.

ready to felt Once the overlapping felt is folded in, the handle attached and the w thing wetted, roll the bag in bubble wrap or a bamboo mat and begin felting.

Hints

To help reinforce the edge of the bag, cut a donut shape from a piece of pre-felt, about 35 cm (14 in) wide and with a 12 cm (4½ in) central hole.

To add decoration to a bag, put the pattern down first, on top of the bamboo mat or bubble wrap. Then layer sliver on top of the pattern, then the template, and proceed as instructed. To decorate the beret, however (which is constructed inside out), lay the design on the layer that precedes the template.

1 Cut a circular template from bubble wrap, about 40 cm (16 in) in diameter. Cut a reinforcing piece of pre-felt (see left).

2 Lay out four or five layers of sliver, about 7 cm (2¾ in) larger than the template all round. Wet the pile (no closer than 7 cm/ 2¾ in to the edge). Put the template on top, then the circle of pre-felt.

3 Fold in the edges, and build more sliver onto them, laying extra around the inside of the circle. The hole in the middle should be between one-half and one-third of the diameter of the pile; because felt shrinks as it is fulled, the holes actually get bigger.

4 For the handle, take two pieces of sliver; their length should be about two-thirds the diameter of the bag. Put them together (parallel), fold in half, and holding them by the ends, dip the middle part in warm soapy water. Pat this middle bit together a little. Spread the soft (dry) ends slightly, then lay the handle across the bag. Lay some extra sliver across the soft ends to strengthen the join. If you wish to wrap the handle with thread (see page 31), this needs to be done before the handle is wetted.

5 Dampen the whole, and begin felting by patting with the hands. When the parcel is nicely wetted and beginning to bond, roll it

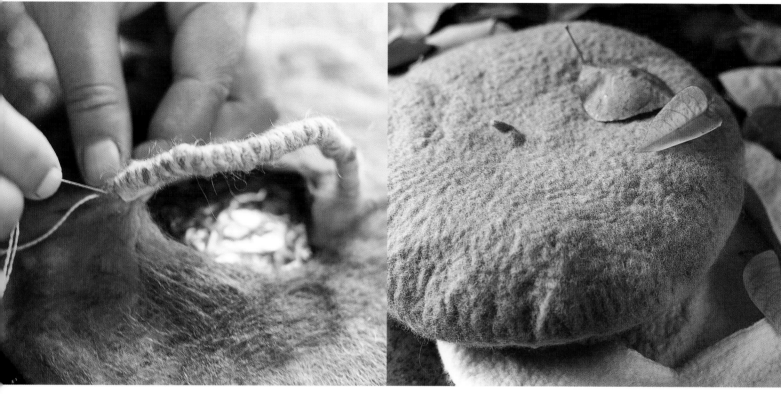

trouble-shooting If the wool is not bonding satisfactorily, you can pull it together with a few stitches.

beret variation A smaller version of the bag, minus the handle and the pre-felt reinforcement, makes a beret. Add a little tail to the top for decoration if you wish.

in a bamboo mat or bubble wrap, changing directions and turning over frequently until the template begins to wrinkle.

6 Remove the template, turn the bag right side out and continue fulling. If you wish to deepen the shape, you can mould the bag by gently pushing with your fist from the inside against a firm surface such as the draining ridges of the kitchen sink.

7 Continue rolling and moulding until the texture is nice and strong, then rinse and dry. When drying, first line the bag with a plastic shopping bag, then stuff with newspaper or more plastic shopping bags.

Variation: beret

Build up three layers of fine wool sliver, the first in a radiating pattern, the second circular and the third radiating. This will avoid ridged areas at the edge of the beret. Wet the wool. Lay a bubble-wrap template (sizes are given on page 28) on top, and fold in the edges. Lay on extra wool so that the hole is about one-third of the diameter of the template; it will become larger as you proceed. Felt as for the pod bag, turning inside out when the template is removed. Shape a little edge for the hole. Allow to dry; then, if desired, stitch some petersham ribbon around the inner edge.

Wrapped handle

To decorate and strengthen the handle, it can be wrapped using wool thread. Do this before the parcel is wetted and felted. Wrap the thread around the handle, or stitch it on using blanket stitch, then fasten off securely, leaving 7–8 cm (about 3 in) fluffy sliver at each end. Dampen the handle in the middle, where it is wrapped. Roll this part between the palms to firm it. Then lay the handle on the bag, roll the whole up in a bamboo mat or bubble wrap and felt in the usual manner.

Honeycomb shawl

The honeycomb shawl is one of the easiest projects to make, as it relies on the creation of felt with interesting holes in it, and can be made in crazy irregular shapes. The beauty of the honeycomb shawl is that no two shawls will ever be exactly alike.

Use the finest Merino sliver for a soft, cuddly wrap. The shawl can be made in one colour, or try varying the colours at random during the layout stage. The edge can be beaded if desired.

Materials
Fine Merino sliver

Tools
Large bamboo mat, approximately 120 x 240 cm (4 x 8 ft)
Soap
Vinegar, for rinsing

Size
Approximately 90 x 210 cm (35½ x 82½ in)

step two Lay strips of sliver in a lattice pattern onto the bamboo mat.

variation one If you wish to create a warmer shawl, lay fine wisps of sliver over the lattice to give a slightly opaque effect, with thinner areas.

1 Have the bamboo mat mostly rolled up. The task of laying out the shawl will be easier if you do it in small sections, working on about 60 cm (24 in) at a time, wetting each section and rolling it up as you go, and unrolling more mat as needed.

2 Pull about 40 cm (16 in) sliver from the roll at a time. Split this lengthways into four to six long pieces. Lay them on the mat, crossing them over each other. If using different colours, interweave them at intervals. Continue in this manner, building up a crisscross or lattice pattern on the mat. The holes, or blank spaces, should be no more than 10 cm (4 in) in diameter, or

the shawl will not be warm. You may like to have a more solid area in the middle of the shawl, to make a warmer garment. In this case, simply fill in the holes with wisps of wool plucked from the sliver. The finished effect will be gauzy areas interspersed with more opaque parts formed by the lattice. (For another variation, make round holes in the gauzy areas, as shown in the photograph opposite). As you complete one part of the shawl, roll up that section of the mat and continue working from the exposed edges.

3 When the layout is complete, and the mat fully rolled up, soak the mat with warm soapy water by pouring it on top, along the

variation two After wetting the sliver, use your fingers to make holes in the wispy areas between the lattice.

diagram 1 Side view of the bamboo blind; the arrows show the direction of the stretch.

whole length. Pat the mat firmly a few times, to help the water travel through all the layers.

4 Leaving a part of the mat (about 20 cm/ 8 in) flat on the work surface, roll the mat back and forth about 50 times. Re-roll the mat, rolling one side up while the other side is being unrolled. If any wrinkles appear, stretch them out by gently pulling the two rolls apart (see Diagram 1).

5 Roll back and forth about 50 times more. Carefully unroll, then pick up a corner of the felt to see if it is strong enough to hold its own wet weight. Once the felt seems

strong enough, carefully gather it together. Lifting and gently dropping the shawl onto the bamboo mat will begin the fulling process. You can alternate the lifting and dropping with gentle kneading. Every now and then, the felt should be spread out to make sure that it is not bonding with itself in surprise places. You may like to gently stretch and shape the shawl during this time. Firm the edges from time to time by working the edge with lightly soaped fingers. The felt will be finished when the fibres have all bonded and the surface is not fluffy. Rinse thoroughly, finishing with a vinegar and water rinse. Dry in the shade. Press with a hot iron if necessary (see right).

Pressing

If you wish to press the shawl, do not move the iron back and forth, as it will catch in the holes. Instead, hold the iron on one section for a few seconds, then lift it and move it to another section. Alternatively, use a pressing cloth (even a sheet of brown paper will do).

Antarctic hat

The fleece of alpacas, a relative of the llama, yields a luxury fibre that is lighter, softer and warmer than sheep's wool, and which has a silky lustre. Its natural colours are black, brown, fawn, grey and white, but dyed raw fleece or processed fibre can also be bought in a range of colours. This quirky, reversible hat uses both wool and alpaca in two colours. Alpaca fibre is naturally lighter on the ends, giving a mottled effect to the surface of the felt. Alternatively, make the hat using all wool sliver.

Made in a smaller size, this is a cute hat for a child. Alpaca fleece shrinks by only 16 per cent when felted, so to work out how to resize the template for a smaller or larger head, measure the head of the intended wearer, divide by two then add 16 per cent. This is the size to which the template needs to be cut.

Materials
Brown alpaca fleece; if you buy raw alpaca fleece (that is, fleece as shorn from the animal's body, without being treated in any way) it must be carded (see page 9) before use
Orange wool sliver
Wool or other thread, for embellishment (optional)

Tools
Bubble wrap
Soap
Towel
Scissors

Size
To fit adult (circumference of brim 56 cm/22 in)

step two Put one layer of brown alpaca fleece on the template, allowing overlap at all edges except the brim edge, then put two layers of orange wool sliver on top.

step three Turn the hat over, add another layer of brown alpaca fleece, then fold in the overlapping edges of the brown alpaca fleece.

1 Using the same template as for the Mammoth tea cosy (see page 100), minus the little peak at the top, cut bubble wrap to make the template.

2 Put one layer of brown alpaca fleece on the template, allowing 7 cm (2¾ in) overlap around the edges, except at the brim edge. Add two medium-thick layers of orange sliver, each at right angles to the previous layer. Sprinkle with warm soapy water and press gently with soapy hands to make sure that all the fibres are wet. Stroke and massage gently until soft felt forms.

3 Turn the whole thing over and add one layer of alpaca, covering only the area of the template. Fold in the overlapping edges.

4 Fold in the overlapping orange wool. Add two medium-thick layers of orange sliver, each at right angles to the previous layer, allowing 7 cm (2¾ in) overlap around all the edges, except at the brim edge as before. Sprinkle with warm soapy water and press gently with soapy hands to ensure all the fibres are wet. Tuck in any sliver that is sticking out. Stroke and massage both sides until soft felt forms, then increase the pressure and hard felt, so that the two edges bond. This will take about 15 minutes.

step four After folding the overlapping edges of the orange wool sliver inwards, add another two layers of orange sliver, then fold in the overlapping edges.

step five Put one hand inside the hat and stroke along the join with your other hand to prevent a ridge forming.

5 Put your hand inside the hat and stroke along the join with your other hand to prevent a ridge forming.

6 Turn the hat inside out and felt until the two pieces are well attached at the edge. Stroke along the join at intervals to prevent a ridge from forming. Immerse the hat in warm water, then grasp and squeeze 50 times vertically then 50 times horizontally.

7 Do the pinch test (see right); if you can grasp single fibres from the felt, the hat will need more massaging. Once the hat is well felted, roll it in a towel to remove excess water (do not wring it), then stretch the felt in both directions so that it is smooth and even. Allow to dry in shade.

8 When completely dry, cut the front to suit the shape of your face. If desired, stitch along the edge of the brim for decoration, as shown in the pictured example.

Variation

Put fleece curls along the lower part of the hat, before beginning to layer the sliver. Then, rather than cutting the brim, turn it up so that the curly fleece forms a contrast with the smooth felt (see page 6).

The pinch test

The pinch test is a useful way of determining whether your felt is adequately fulled. Pinch the felt between your fingertips; if you can grasp single fibres from the felt, it needs more fulling. Keep massaging until it passes the pinch test; this will ensure a firm and durable felt.

Shaggy rug with fleece curls

This rug has a surface layer felted from raw (unprocessed) fleece. Try to find wool from Leicester Longwool (used in the pictured example), Lincoln, Friesian, Wensleydale or other lustre-wool breeds that have a long staple (see page 10). Adult wool will have the longest, strongest locks; lambs' fleeces will make a soft rug, ideal for a bedroom and bare feet. The raw fleece may look and feel a little dirty; however, it will soften and become clean during the felting process.

Materials

Raw fleece curls, such as Leicester Longwool
Wool sliver: strong Merino (over 22 microns)
   or a medium crossbreed of 25–28 microns

Tools

Large bamboo blind
Plastic fly-wire
Plastic shopping bag
Soap
Cotton rag, for tying the felting roll
Vinegar, for rinsing

Size

Approximately 70 x 180 cm (27½ x 71 in)

step one Spread the curls of raw fleece (here, Leicester Longwool) on the bamboo blind, removing any seeds or foreign matter.

step two Cover the fleece curls with several layers of reasonably strong sliver, each layer at right angles to the former.

1 Spread the unwashed fleece evenly across a large bamboo blind. If you spot any grass-seeds or other foreign bodies, remove them. If space is a problem, the rug can be laid out and rolled up in sections. It doesn't matter if the fibres are going in all different directions on this layer, as there will be substantial layers of felt forming the backing.

2 Over this layer, lay a reasonably strong Merino or medium crossbreed sliver to help bond the fleece curls. The rug will need at least four layers of wool at right angles to each other, in addition to the surface layer.

3 Because the rug will be quite thick, it is helpful to sprinkle the layers with water as you build them up. However, because wool 'relaxes' and remembers its original structure when wet, it is important not to leave a carpet half-finished and damp overnight. In the morning, the damp fibres will have regained their original curl, which may affect the design.

4 When the rug is fully laid out and wetted, lay a sheet of plastic fly-wire across the top. Using a scrunched-up plastic bag, and working in sections, rub gently across the surface in a circular motion to remove air bubbles and spread the moisture evenly

Flipping the rug Flip the heavy, wet felt safely and easily by reverse-rolling it (see Hints, right).

Checking progress Unroll the flipped rug to inspect the surface. Pick out any seeds that have come to the surface, and continue to roll until of a satisfactory firmness.

throughout. It may help to rub a bar of soap lightly across the fly-wire, and then sprinkle with more water. When the air bubbles have been released and the fibres are wet, tightly roll the bamboo blind, lifting it slightly as you roll, so that water or air bubbles underneath can escape. Tie the roll firmly in three or four places, using strips of cotton rag (the knots are less likely to work loose than if you use string).

5 The rug must now be rolled back and forth about 200 times, before unrolling and reversing the direction. It may be rolled with the arms on a bench, or placed on the floor and rolled with the feet, from a standing or sitting position. If working outside on a paved area, it is wise to wrap the bamboo roll in an old sheet, tying it off securely before rolling, in order to protect the bamboo blind from damage.

6 When the rug has been rolled 200 times from each direction (a total of 400 rolls), it should be turned over and the process repeated. After a further 2 x 200 rolls, the rug should be of a sturdy texture, and can be thoroughly rinsed and dried flat. Add half a cup of white vinegar to the final rinsing water. Vinegar is an acid and counters the alkalinity of the soap, acting as a conditioner.

Hints

To flip a heavy, wet article such as this rug, reverse-roll it. Take the front edge of the bamboo blind and roll it under, towards you, carefully rolling the felt with it. When the whole roll is unrolled again, the blind will have flipped.

Champagne cooler

This Champagne cooler is made in two parts. The inner sleeve is fitted to the bottle and provides a base; the outer sleeve, which can be made as thick as you wish, is both decorative and insulating. For picnic portability, add a carry-strap. The template can be sized to suit any type of bottle. Such a cooler is excellent for a water-bottle, with or without a carry-strap; the felt will keep a pre-frozen drink cool for hours.

Materials
Wool sliver
Buttons, beads and thread, for embellishment
  (optional)

Tools
Used Champagne or other bottle
Bubble wrap, for template
Bamboo mat or bubble wrap, for rolling
Chalk
Soap
Towel

inner sleeve, step one Once the layers of wool are laid out on the marked area of the bamboo mat or bubble wrap, moisten the central section only.

inner sleeve, step two Lay the template on the central section of the wool, pressing down gently to remove any air bubbles.

Making the template

Measure the circumference of your chosen bottle, add 50 per cent (to allow for shrinkage of one-third) and divide the total by 2 to give you the width of your template. Decide how tall you wish your cooler to be, and add 50 per cent to give the height. Cut a template from bubble wrap, about 15 cm (6 in) longer than the required height and exactly the width you have calculated. Mark the required height with a waterproof marker.

INNER SLEEVE

1 Make a template (see left). Then lay the template on the bamboo mat or bubble wrap that you will use for rolling the felt. Using chalk, draw a line around the template, about 8 cm (3¼ in) away from the edge, marking the height required. Put the template aside, then lay out three or four layers of sliver at right angles to each other, filling out to the edges of the chalked line. Carefully sprinkle the middle of the wool pile with warm soapy water, using the template as a guide. It is important not to wet the sides, or they will become difficult to handle.

2 Lay the bubble wrap template on the wool, pressing down gently (but without popping the cells). Pat the template using the fingertips to gently push out any air bubbles from the wool.

3 Very carefully fold the edges of the wool up and inwards, over the edges of the template and towards the middle. Sprinkle them gently with water as you go, so that they don't spring back. Fill in the middle of the template with as many layers of wool as were used underneath, making sure all the layers overlap. Sprinkle the whole with warm water.

inner sleeve, step three Fold the edges of the wool inwards, over the sides of the template and towards the middle.

inner sleeve, step three continued Fill in the middle of the template with as many layers of wool as were used on the first side.

4 Taking a bar of soap, gently soap your wet hands. Begin to carefully pat the soap on to the wool. You will notice the felting process beginning. Re-soaping your hands frequently, make sure the surface of the parcel is soaped and wetted out. Carefully turn the pile over and repeat.

5 When you are sure that both sides are wetted out and there are no air bubbles in the wool, roll the parcel up gently in the bamboo mat. Roll it about 20 times, not pressing down too hard. Unroll and repeat from the other direction. Keep repeating this process, changing the direction of the little woolly parcel within the mat.

6 Keep note of the edges of the parcel, and keep smoothing around the edges of the template with your hands. When the felt feels strong enough, remove the template and turn the sleeve inside out. Continue to full the felt by gentle kneading, rolling and dropping; you can also shock the felt (see right) if you wish. Insert the bottle and rub the felt gently, forming it to the shape of the bottle, remembering to leave the neck of the cooler open so that the bottle can be removed. Massage the bottom of the felt pocket so that it forms to the punt (the indentation at the base of the bottle). Rinse and set aside, leaving the pocket on the bottle for now.

'Shocking' the felt

You can hasten the process of felting by dipping the felt alternately in very hot and very cold water. This is called 'shocking' the felt and will make it quite tough.

inner sleeve, step six When the felt is strong enough, remove the template, turn the sleeve inside out and continue fulling. Soap any loose areas to help them felt.

inner sleeve, step six continued To help full the sleeve, stuff it with a rolled piece of bubble wrap, to keep the shape while maintaining malleability for kneading.

OUTER SLEEVE

1 Next, lay out a piece of flat felt, at least four layers in thickness, 60–90 cm (24–36 in) long (depending how much insulation you desire). If you require thicker felt, you may like to cut the sliver for the inner layers into short lengths of about 2.5 cm (1 in), which will allow you to build up a thicker felt without the difficulty of the layers sliding away over each other.

2 If making a thicker felt, it must be very thoroughly wetted out and the felting begun using applied pressure through a piece of plastic fly-wire, nylon netting or non-slip matting. You can begin to roll it when you feel it firming up under your hands. You may like to build the edges out of layers of different coloured sliver, so that a small rainbow detail emerges when the edge is trimmed. After the felt is wetted, fold in about 2 cm (¾ in) at each end (the two short sides) and pat them down. This will strengthen and neaten the edge.

3 When the felt is crisp and firm, gently press the water out using a towel (do not wring the felt), then trim the two long edges, using the stitching-lines on the bamboo mat as a guide. Wrap the long piece of felt around the bottle, and trim the top edge of the inner pocket level with the

inner sleeve, step 6 continued Put the sleeve on the bottle. Pressing with your fingers, form its base to the shape of the indentation on the bottom of the bottle.

variation A miniature version of the Champagne-cooler template can be used to create a mobile-phone pouch.

wrapped sleeve. Allow the felt to dry, then remove the bottle and secure the two layers to each other using buttons, beads or a few decorative stitches.

Variation: phone pouch

A mini version of the wine-cooler template can be used to make a mobile-phone pouch. Cut a rectangular template (you can use cardboard rather than bubble wrap; it will become soggy, but can be discarded after use) about 20 x 10 cm (8 x 4 in). Trim the corners so that they are curved. Felt around the template, following the instructions for the inner sleeve. When sufficiently firm,

cut a slit in one side of the felt, about 4 cm (1½ in) along from one of the shorter edges and about 2 cm (¾ in) in from each of the longer edges. Remove the template and continue felting, encouraging the short part above the slit to felt together and become one thickish layer. Make sure the two sides of the pouch don't stick together elsewhere. Felt it to a size that fits your mobile phone (wrap the phone in protective plastic before inserting it into the wet felt to try it for size), then rinse and allow to dry. Attach a decorative cord to the firm top edge of the pouch, and decorate the felt with a little embroidery or beading if desired for a cute little phone pouch.

Soft cloche hat

This hat is shaped like a bell, hence its name;

cloche is French for bell. Fitted hats such as

cloches normally need to be formed on a hat

block; as this is not something that most people

have, this hat is made from a bubble-wrap

template tailored to the head of the wearer.

The beauty of the bubble-wrap template is that

you can cut virtually any shape you like, with

spikes and blobs, extended crowns and brims,

and then felt it.

Materials
Merino sliver

Tools
Bubble wrap, for template
Scissors
Bamboo mat or bubble wrap, for rolling
Soap
Towel

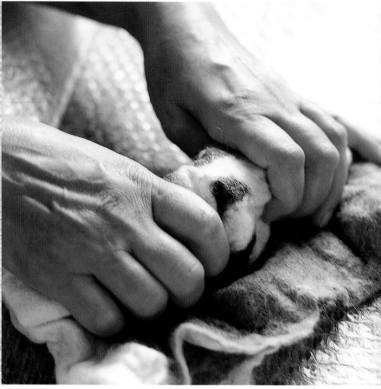

step three Press down gently on the bubble-wrap template to ensure that there are no air bubbles underneath it.

step four Once the hat is soft-felted, roll it up on itself and roll it back and forth about 20 rolls at a time, checking on the edges and seams as you go.

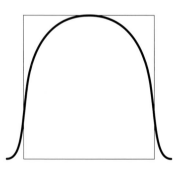

The template is formed from a rectangle calculated on your own head size, which then is rounded off at the top corners and widened at the bottom into a bell shape.

1 To make a hat blocked (formed) on your own or another's head (in the absence of a hat block), you will need to make a template. Measure around the head, add 50 per cent of the measurement and then divide the total by 2, to give you the width of the template. Then measure from the centre crown to the middle of the ear, add 50 per cent of the measurement, and divide the total by 2, to give you the height of the template. Draw a rectangle using the height and width you have calculated. Trim the top corners to curves and very slightly widen the bottom edge so that you have a sort of bell shape (see Diagram 1). Cut out a template to this shape from bubble wrap.

2 Trace around the outside of the template onto the mat or the bubble wrap in which you will roll the felt, adding about 7 cm (2¾ in) around the edge, except at the brim edge. Remove the template, then, using the traced line as a guide, lay out sliver in four thin layers. Reinforce the brim slightly by laying a little extra sliver along the edge.

3 Sprinkle the middle of the layers with warm soapy water. Lay the template on top, pressing down gently to remove air bubbles. Fold the edges of the wool in over the template, and fill in the middle of the template so that the thickness of wool is even over the whole. Remember to create a

the finished 'hood' The felt is now ready for blocking or shaping.

variation The crown of the hat can be depressed to give a different shape.
A ribbon or a felt rope, as shown, can be tied around the base for decoration.

slight overlap with the folded-in edges, and to repeat the reinforcement of the brim.

4 Wet the whole parcel, and begin the felting process by patting it gently with the fingers. Pay attention to the edges of the template, watching for holes and making sure that no ridges form. If they do, smooth them out with the fingers. Then roll the hat, about 20 rolls at a time, checking the edges and seams in between each set of rolls.

5 When the felt is strong enough to turn over, firm the brim edge of the hat. Soap the fingers and very gently rub the edges of the felt, using a circular motion and about the same pressure one would use for washing one's face. You will notice the felt visibly shrinking and firming.

6 Once the hat begins to exert pressure on the template, remove the template. You can now start to full quite vigorously, rolling the hat between the hands, dropping, dipping in hot and cold water, and rolling it on the mat. Try the hat on from time to time, to make sure it doesn't become too small. When it reaches the required size, rinse in warm water, press out in a towel (do not wring) and put it on, smoothing it and shaping the edge. Line with a plastic shopping bag, stuff with crumpled newspaper and leave to dry.

Hint

When laying out the sliver to form the hat, remember that several thin layers are better than fewer thick ones, making a stronger and more even felt. The finer the sliver you use, the softer the hat, which is why high-quality Merino is specified. If you wish to use stronger wool, the hat may need to be lined with silk or cotton fabric, to prevent an itch problem.

Cobweb scarf

Cobweb scarves are very fine and delicate but beautifully warm, as they trap warm air around the body. The pictured example has wisps of soy silk laid down first for embellishment.

This project will require its own room for a few hours; as the shawl is so fine, it is best laid out in a room where there will be no sudden drafts of air to waft away the sliver. Also, it needs to rest for a couple of hours, so construct it somewhere where pets or other people cannot disturb it.

Sliver can be prepared for cobweb felting well in advance. Spread it in sections using butter paper or waxed lunchwrap to support it, rolling it up as you go for use later on.

Materials
Fiine Merino sliver
Soy silk or other fibres for embellishment
   (optional; see page 57)

Tools
Bubble wrap, about 2.5 m x 40 cm
   (98½ x 16 in)
Hand-mister
Towel
Soap

Size
Approximately 40 x 150 cm (16 x 59 in)

Note
The finished scarf will be wider than the sliver
   that is originally laid out. This is because
   there is no lateral bonding of the fibres, as
   they are all laid out longitudinally, so the
   scarf can actually spread sideways during
   the felting process. It will only decrease in
   size lengthways

Calculating quantities

It is difficult to give precise quantities of sliver required for felting projects, as the same volume of wool from different breeds will have different weights; for example, a bag made of Leicester or Lincoln could weigh at least half as much again as one of a similar size and thickness of felt made from Merino. The following rough guidelines may be helpful, however.

A lightweight shawl measuring approximately 90 x 180 cm (35½ x 71 in) might require 300–500 g (10½ oz–17½ oz), depending on its thickness and pattern. If making 'nuno' felt (using a woven backing), you can get away with as little as 100 g (3½ oz), if using fine Merino sliver. A heavy rug might need as much as 700 g–1 kg (1 lb 9 oz–2 lb 4 oz). It is safest to buy more rather than less; any leftovers can be used to create pre-felts or to make decorations for other projects.

step two Carefully spread out the sliver laterally into a fine, even layer about 30 cm (12 in) wide.

1 Lay the bubble wrap on a long table or on the floor, bubble side down. Take a length of wool sliver about 2.5 m (98½ in) long and lay it along the length of the bubble wrap.

2 Very carefully begin to pull the sliver laterally, spreading the fibres without pulling them apart lengthways. Work slowly and carefully so that the fibres will be spread evenly across the bubble wrap. You should be able to spread them about 30 cm (12 in) wide. They will look quite delicate and thin.

3 Using a hand-mister, gently mist the spread wool sliver along its whole length, using *cold* slightly soapy water. Once it is

completely misted, leave it undisturbed for at least two hours, or preferably overnight.

4 After two hours, you will see that the wool fibres will have relaxed under moisture, that they will be quite wavy, and that a lacy pattern will have begun to appear. Gently sprinkle all of the wool with warm, slightly soapy water. Carefully roll up the bubble wrap, and very lightly begin to squeeze the bundle. Gently roll it back and forth. Re-roll in the other direction, and repeat the process. Cobweb felt must be made slowly and gently as it has a delicate and fragile textile.

Using templates

Many felted items require a template made from bubble wrap (or a similar recyclable flexible non-stick material). Flat objects such as scarves do not need a template. The felt for a three-dimensional object such as a bag is made around both sides of the template. For some items, the template is laid down first, then the sliver put on top; for others, the sliver is laid out first, then the template added. As you become adept at felting, you will be able to choose which method is most appropriate for the item you are making.

When using a template, chalk its outline on the bamboo mat or bubble wrap. Use this as a guide when laying down the sliver, allowing sufficient sliver (7–10 cm/2¾–4 in) to fold over the edge. Once the wool is laid out, wet the centre area, making sure the edges to be folded remain dry. Lay the template down, patting firmly from the middle outwards to ensure wetting and to remove air bubbles. Fold in the edges, fill in the remaining area to the same thickness as the rest, and proceed with felting.

When using a template you may choose to make the article 'inside out', as it is easier to make decorative designs stay exactly where you want them. Also, any solid ridges at the edges can be trimmed or hidden on the inside of the item.

step four Make sure the wool is thoroughly wetted before rolling up the bundle.

5 The felt may also be helped along by slipping two large elastic bands around the rolled bubble wrap, and simply picking up and dropping the whole bundle a few times. In fact, if the bundle is well secured, it can be kicked gently around the floor as the felt gets stronger. After an hour or so of gentle massage, rolling and dropping (re-rolling the work from time to time to ensure even felting), remove the felt from the bubble wrap and gently rinse in lukewarm water. Place in a towel, roll up, and then place the rolled towel on the floor. Stand on the towel a few times to squeeze the moisture out of the felt (never wring the felt). Unroll and allow the felt to dry in the shade.

Variations

Once the sliver has been laid out, and before the misting, small scraps of silk and wool threads and yarns can be added to the scarf, either at random or laid as a pattern. You can even add soft feathers if you wish. (These embellishments can be laid at right angles to or parallel with the sliver, as you wish; each way will create a slightly different look.) Then felt as described above.

To encourage bigger holes in your cobweb felt, use the fingering technique in Step 2 of the Honeycomb shawl (see pages 34–35).

Kimono collar

For this project, you will need curly wool from one of the lustre-wool breeds. Leicester, Lincoln and Romney are available in Australia. In North America, look for Leicester, Cotswold, Romney, Finn and Swaledale. In Britain, you will be able to obtain Wensleydale, Teeswater and many other delightful breeds. In the rest of Europe, use lambs' curls from breeds such as Gotland or Friesian. As the collar will be worn next to the skin, use the finest Merino sliver for the body of the collar, to create a very soft felt.

You could also try the hair from Angora rabbits or Mohair goats. Alternatively, use locks from adult sheep of the breeds described, but be aware that they may feel a bit rough.

Materials
Curly orange wool (the pictured example
 uses Leicester Longwool)
Fine beige Merino sliver
Felted toggle (see page 61), purchased toggle
 or long button
Bead (optional)
Wool yarn, for attaching toggle

Tools
Bubble wrap
Scissors
Watering can
Soap
Towel

Size
Approximately 80 x 14 cm (31½ x 5½ in),
 excluding fringe

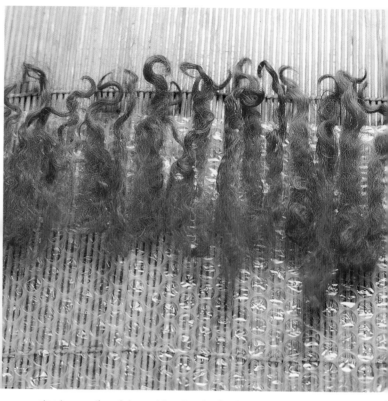

step two Cut the raw fleece curls into pieces about 13 cm (5 in) long. There is no need to be exact; some variation in length will add visual interest.

step two continued Lay out the strands of curly wool on bubble wrap, so that they all face in the same direction. Stagger the cut ends to give a more interesting effect.

Hint

Different looks can be achieved according to the order in which you put down the layers. For a mottled effect, in which the colours of the curly and plain fleeces meld (see page 59), sandwich the curly fleece between two layers of plain sliver. This produces the same look on both sides of the collar. Alternatively, lay down the curly fleece first, then top it with two layers of sliver, as in the step photographs above. This produces a different look on each side of the collar.

1 Cut a piece of bubble wrap 85 x 16 cm (33½ x 6¼ in) for the template.

2 Cut the curly wool into pieces about 13 cm (5 in) long. Lay them along one edge of the bubble wrap, allowing the curly ends to protrude beyond the bubble wrap by about 6 cm (2½ in), and placing all the pieces so they face in the same direction.

3 Put two layers of beige sliver at right angles to each other on top of the curly wool, leaving the curly ends free, and covering the entire piece of bubble wrap with sliver (you do not need to allow any overlap at the edges).

4 Using a watering can, gently sprinkle the whole with warm soapy water. Press the wool all over with your palm until it is evenly wetted and the air bubbles are pressed out. Stroke in each direction very gently (as though giving a baby its first bath) to make the surface of the felt flat. Using your fingertips, make the inner (non-curly) edge and the ends of the collar round and firm by turning under any bits of wool that are sticking out and gently massaging the edge. When you feel the felt begin to harden a little, you can apply more pressure.

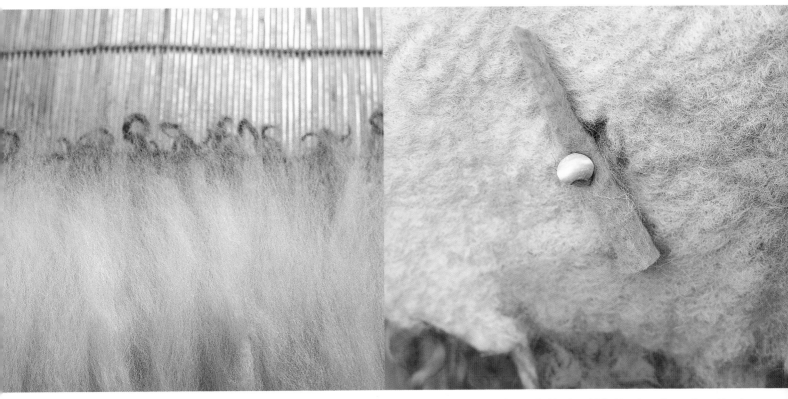

step three Cover the cut ends of the curly wool with two layers of sliver, leaving the curly ends free.

detail The collar is fastened with a hand-felted toggle and a purchased bead. A purchased long button can be used instead.

5 Massage for about 5 minutes, until the orange and beige fibres begin to intermingle (this indicates that the item is felting well). Then turn the whole thing over, sprinkle with more warm soapy water and massage for 5 minutes more in each direction. Then immerse the felt in hot water and grasp and squeeze it about 50 times in each direction. Transfer to cold water and grasp and squeeze 50 times more in each direction.

6 Put the felt on a flat surface and sprinkle with warm soapy water. Keep massaging on both sides for about 10 minutes in total, then grasp and squeeze 50 times in each direction. Do the pinch test (see page 39);

if the felt is not adequately fulled, it will need more massaging.

7 Roll the felt in a towel to remove excess water (do not wring it), then stretch it in both directions. Dry flat and in shade.

8 When the collar is completely dry, try it on and mark the position for the toggle and buttonhole. Using scissors, cut a slit for the buttonhole. Sew on the toggle, adding a bead if desired, as in the pictured example.

Felted toggle

The toggle on the pictured collar is made from a tapered roll of sliver that has been felted, allowed to dry then cut across the thicker end.

Patchwork blanket

This blanket can be made in a very small house or apartment, as it is constructed from small pre-felts made with a sushi mat. These are then sewn together and the blanket is felted in the bath or shower.

Materials
Wool sliver in various colours, for making pre-felts

Wool yarn

Tools
Bamboo sushi mat, for making pre-felts

Darning needle

Large bamboo mat (optional)

Vinegar, for rinsing

1 Using a variety of colours, make a range of fairly firm, small pre-felts using a bamboo sushi mat at the kitchen table or sink. You may like to introduce simple patterns or designs. Use two layers of wool sliver, laid at right angles to each other, in addition to the design layer. All of the pre-felts should be of similar texture, as it is more difficult to bond felts of dissimilar strength. You will need about 30 pre-felts for a baby rug, or as many as 600 for a large bed blanket.

2 Sew the pre-felts together using a large darning needle and wool yarn in a matching or contrasting shade. Overlap the patches slightly, and allow the blanket to grow in an organic fashion. You can use large or small stitches, in running, cross or seed and/or chain stitch. In the end, all of the stitches will be felted into the blanket, becoming part of the surface. If there are odd-shaped gaps, fill them with small pre-felt shapes and a few interesting stitches.

3 When all of the patches are stitched together, take the blanket to the bath or shower. Wet it thoroughly with warm soapy water, and roll and drop-full it until the felt is the firmness you want. If you have the space, roll the blanket in a large bamboo mat; this process allows more control over felting and makes the felt crisper.

4 If you have a front-loading washing machine, and the blanket is not too big, you can complete the felting by washing the blanket on a wool or handwash cycle, after you have begun the process in the bath. Be aware, though, that the washing machine is a most efficient felting tool, and that things can rapidly get out of hand. Felt fulled in a machine tends to be fluffier than felt fulled by rolling in a mat or bubble wrap.

5 When it is fully felted, rinse thoroughly, finishing with a water and vinegar rinse. Spin excess water out, and dry in shade.

Variations

Make the squares using butter muslin (a very open-weave muslin) or cheesecloth and wool for a very lightweight blanket.

Make all of the squares in white wool, and overdye the pre-felts using shibori techniques before stitching.

Add decorations such as beads and buttons, or even small pockets for secret notes.

For a truly warm and cuddly baby blanket, line the felted blanket with soft silk cloth, simply tacking it to the back by hand.

Reverse inlay rug

The design on this boldly patterned rug is laid out from the front surface back. While this means you won't see the pattern properly until the first time you turn the felt over, its advantage is that the pattern will be well bonded with the rest of the rug. Layers of sliver are built up on top of the design to give a sturdy and hard-wearing rug.

If planning a complicated design, you could rough it out on a large sheet of paper first and use this as a guide when laying out. If you have more experience or confidence, lay the pieces straight onto the bamboo mat, rearranging them to your satisfaction before laying sliver on top.

The same technique, with more layers of wool, can be used to create a bathmat (see page 67).

Materials
Pieces of sliver, loose fleece or shapes cut
    from pre-felt, for the inlay pattern
Wool sliver

Tools
Bubble wrap
Large bamboo blind
Chalk
Plastic fly-wire
Plastic shopping bag
Soap
Strips of cotton rag, for tying

step two Begin to build up the pattern on the bamboo blind, working from the front to the back of the rug.

step three Infill the design with sliver, building up four layers and ensuring there is an even thickness across the whole rug.

Calculating dimensions

Layout area	Approximate finished size
90 x 90 cm (35½ x 35½ in)	60 x 60 cm (24 x 24 in)
120 x 180 cm (47 x 71 in)	80 x 120 cm (31½ x 47 in)
150 x 150 cm (59 x 59 in)	100 x 100 cm (39½ x 39½ in)

1 Chalk your design onto the bamboo mat. Remember that the finished felt will only be two-thirds the area of the laid-out fleece. The layout should equal the desired finished size plus 50 per cent. The chart at left may be helpful.

2 Lay out the pattern, working from the 'top' (the front surface) back. You can cut lengths of sliver, use loose fleece or cut shapes from pre-felt to develop the design for your rug. It doesn't matter that the fibres are going in all different directions on this layer, as there will be substantial layers of felt forming the backing.

3 The rug will need at least four layers of wool, in addition to the design layer. Put each layer of sliver at right angles to the previous, and make sure that the thickness is even across the whole rug. You may find that a 90 x 150 cm (35½ x 59 in) rug will require 1 kg (2 lb 4 oz) of wool. It is helpful to sprinkle the layers with water as you build them up. However, it is important not to leave a rug half-finished and damp overnight, as wool has a 'memory'; in the morning, the damp fibres will have regained their original curl (which was straightened during combing and carding), and this may affect the design.

step five After the rug has been rolled 200 times in each direction, unroll it to reveal the design. Then re-roll the parcel and roll it back and forth a further 2 x 200 times.

variation A sturdy bathmat (tailored to the size and shape of your bathroom floor, if you like) can be created using the same technique, with or without a pattern.

4 When the rug is fully laid out and wetted, lay a sheet of plastic fly-wire across the top. Using a scrunched-up plastic shopping bag, rub gently across the surface in a circular motion to remove air bubbles and spread the moisture evenly throughout. It may help to rub a bar of soap lightly across the fly-wire, and then sprinkle water over the top again. When the air bubbles have been released and the fibres are wet, tightly roll the mat, lifting it slightly as you roll, so that water or air beneath does not affect the design. Tie the roll firmly in three or four places, using strips of cotton rag (the knots will be less likely to work loose than if you use string).

5 The rug must now be rolled back and forth about 200 times, before unrolling and reversing the direction. It may be rolled on a bench, or placed on the floor and rolled with the feet, from a standing or sitting position. If you wish to work outside on a paved area, it is wise to wrap the bamboo roll in an old sheet, tying it securely, before rolling, to protect the mat from damage. When the rug has been rolled from both directions (a total of 400 rolls), turn it over to show the design, then repeat the rolling process. After a further 2 x 200 rolls, its texture should be sturdy. Rinse thoroughly, adding half a cup of white vinegar to the final rinsing water, then allow to dry flat.

Bathmat variation

For a bathmat, lay out wool about 90 x 60 cm (35½ x 24 in) for a rectangular or oval mat, or 90 x 90 cm (35½ x 35½ in) for a round mat. The mat will need at least six layers of wool, in addition to the design layer. Extra texture may be added by laying whole lengths of sliver into the felt at intervals. Construct and roll the mat as described at left. The bathmat will keep felting throughout its life, becoming firmer and more compact as people walk on it with wet feet.

Origami bag

This sturdy bag is constructed from four squares of pre-made, finished felt folded to give roomy pockets. You can vary the size of the bag by changing the size of the squares you start with. The tote bag pictured here is made from pieces 50 cm (20 in) square. The bag could also be made as a handbag or, if you're really keen, a weekender. Requirements for these other sizes are given on the following pages.

The handles can be varied. Making them from the same flat felt as the body of the bag creates strong handles that will sustain a fair load, such as are suitable for the tote or weekender. For a smaller bag that will carry a lighter load, you could make a handle from a rope of felt.

Materials (for the tote bag)
Completely fulled felt, from which to cut the pieces

Thread for machine-sewing and/or stranded or pearl cotton for hand-sewing

Two felt balls or bobbles (see pages 19–21), or purchased round buttons

Cardboard, for making the insert for the base of the bag (optional)

Tools
Sewing machine

Large sharp or crewel needle

Size
Approximately 35 x 35 x 15 cm (14 x 14 x 6 in), for the tote bag pictured at left; for other sizes, see pages 70 and 71

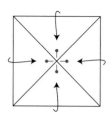

diagram 1 Taking one felt square, fold each corner into the centre and pin in place.

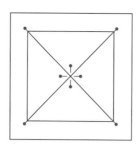

diagram 2 Centre the folded piece on one of the other squares and pin in place.

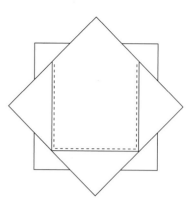

diagram 3 Open out the flaps and sew a little way inside the fold lines along the sides and bottom as shown.

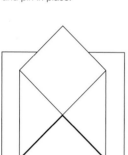

diagram 4 Open out the top flap, then sew together the seams indicated by the bold line.

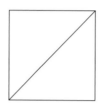

diagram 5 Cut the smaller felt square on the diagonal to make the pocket extension pieces.

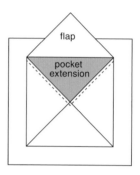

flap

pocket extension

diagram 6 Sew the pocket extension piece behind the pocket formed by the lower three triangles.

To make a handbag

Pocket pieces: four squares 40 x 40 cm (16 x 16 in)

Pocket extension pieces: one square 18 x 18 cm (7 x 7 in), cut in half diagonally

Handles: twine together two pieces of sliver about 1.3 m (51 in) long, wet them with warm soapy water and roll between your hands until firm. This creates a strap about 90 cm (35½ in) long

Button tabs: two pieces 6 x 3 cm (2½ x 1¼ in)

Side straps (optional): two pieces 12 x 2 cm (4½ x ¾ in)

PREPARATION

When cutting pieces from felt, it will be easier to make the felt slightly larger than the required size then trim it to the right shape and size; or make one large sheet of felt and divide it into squares.

You can vary the look of the bag by making either one colour felt, or felt with different colours on either side.

For the pocket pieces, cut four squares of felt 50 x 50 cm (20 x 20 in). It is most important that they all be perfectly square and the same size.

For the pocket extension pieces, cut one square 20 x 20 cm (8 x 8 in). Cut it in half diagonally (see Diagram 5) to give two identical triangles.

For the handles, cut two pieces 50 x 10 cm (20 x 4 in).

For the button tab, cut one piece 12 x 3 cm (4½ x 1¼ in).

For the optional side straps, if using, cut two pieces 12 x 2 cm (4½ x ¾ in).

step two Place one folded and one unfolded square together and stitch along the lines as shown in Diagram 3, using one or two rows of stitching as you prefer.

steps three and four Stitch the lower edges together to form a pocket. Using a flat seam, attach the pocket extension piece to make the pocket deeper.

MAKING THE POCKETS

1 Take one square and fold the corners towards the centre, so that they meet in the middle (see Diagram 1). Pin them down.

2 Pin this (now smaller) square to one of the remaining squares (see Diagram 2), placing the pins at the corners. After they are positioned, open out the flaps (see Diagram 3). Use the dotted line on this diagram as the stitching guide (you can stitch by machine or hand, as you prefer). Stitch slightly in from the fold lines, and don't go too close to the corner, as it becomes too difficult to stitch neatly. Also, the pockets will have a more interesting shape, and will be able to hold wider

objects, if not too closely stitched to the main body of the bag.

3 Fold in the bottom and two side flaps again. Referring to Diagram 4, stitch together the edges marked by a bold line, leaving the top flap free.

4 To finish the pocket, place the pocket extension piece (see Diagram 5) behind the pocket formed by the three lower triangles (see Diagram 6). Using a flat seam, hand-sew the extension piece in place.

Repeat Steps 1–4 with the remaining two squares to make another pocket piece.

To make a weekender

Pocket pieces: four squares 70 x 70 cm (27½ x 27½ in)
Pocket extension pieces: one square 33 x 33 cm (13 x 13 in), cut in half diagonally
Handles: two pieces 30 x 10 cm (12 x 4 in)
Button tabs: two pieces 6 x 3 cm (2½ x 1¼ in)
Side straps (optional): two pieces 15 x 3 cm (6 x 1¼ in)

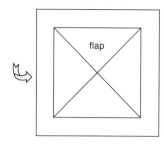
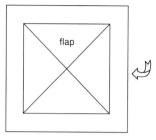

diagram 7 Sew the bottom and sides of the two pocket pieces together, right sides facing.

diagram 8 For the handles, fold each piece of felt in half lengthways, wrong sides together. Sew along the dotted lines, beginning and ending about 9 cm (3½ in) from each short end.

diagram 9 To reinforce, overstitch the ends of the handle seams at the points shown.

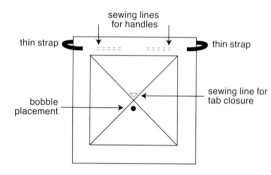

diagram 10 Showing sewing and placement lines for attaching all the components.

Lining

You may wish to line the bag with a woven fabric. Simply stitch a square of your chosen fabric to each felt square before beginning to assemble the bag.

SEWING THE BAG

Place the two pieces with the right (pocket) sides facing each other, making sure that the pocket openings are at the top (see Diagram 7). Stitch them together at both sides and along the bottom. Then taking the bottom corners, stitch diagonally across them about 3 cm (1¼ in) from the corner point, at right angles to the bottom seam. Turn the bag right side out. You will see that it now has a flattish base. You can make this firmer by covering a piece of stiff cardboard in cloth or felt, and placing it in the bottom of the bag. The length of this piece of cardboard should be 8 cm (3¼ in) shorter than the height of the bag.

FINISHING

To make the handles, fold each piece of felt in half lengthways, wrong sides together. Beginning and ending about 9 cm (3½ in) from each short end, sew along the dotted lines indicated in Diagram 8. To reinforce, overstitch several times at the points indicated by the dots (see Diagram 9).

Pin the ends of the handles to the bag, about 5 cm (2 in) down from the top and about 14 cm (5½ in) in from the side seams (see Diagram 10). Before stitching, make sure you are happy with the placement and that the handles are level. Sew by hand, using two lines of stitching.

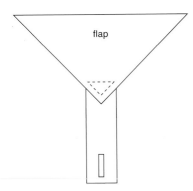

diagram 11 Sew the button tab to the point of the pocket flap, then cut a slit in the end just large enough for the button.

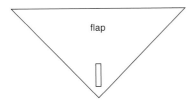

diagram 12 Alternative closure: rather than attaching a button tab, simply cut a slit in the point of the pocket flap.

For the flap closures, make two small felt balls or bobbles (see pages 19–21), and sew them just below the point where the triangles of the outer pockets meet. Sew a button tab to the point of each pocket flap (see Diagram 11). Cut a slit in the other end for the bobble or button. Alternatively, rather than making a button tab, carefully cut a small vertical hole in the point of the overhanging flap, just big enough for the bobble or button to slip through.

You may wish to make small gathers across the top of the side seams and attach small, thin straps, to give the bag a more rounded shape (see Diagram 13).

variation For a handbag, an alternative handle can be made from a rope of felt that is then stitched securely at each side seam.

Variations

When sewing on the outer pockets, simultaneously add inner pockets (this means you will need six squares to begin with). Or, for less bulk inside the bag, cut four squares of felt the same size as the folded squares to make patch pockets.

After placing the pockets and before stitching together the two panels, add a zipper to the top of the big internal pocket by stitching it in, with right sides facing up, while the pieces are flat. Then fold the bag inside out to stitch the side seams.

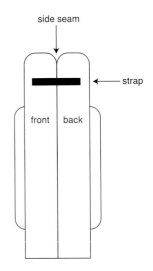

diagram 13 If desired, gather in the sides of the bag a little and secure with a small strap to give the bag a more rounded shape.

Donut pet bed and toy accessories

This cosy, donut-shaped bed will make a snug nest for your cat or dog. The instructions given will make a bed for an average-sized cat or a small dog, but the bed can be tailored to most sizes of pet (see page 77). Alternatively, the bed can be constructed from two flat pieces of felt if desired, and made in any shape you like.

To make your pet's happiness complete, also included are instructions for two simple toys; one formed around a ping-pong ball, the other in the shape of a mouse. They will prove so popular that you may find yourself making frequent replacements!

Materials
Wool sliver
Wool yarn
Stuffing: various materials are suitable,
    including washed fleece, old clothes,
    commercially available polyester fibrefill,
    or odd socks from the washing basket;
    even newspaper will do at a pinch

Tools
Bubble wrap, for template
Large bamboo blind
Chalk
Soap
Plastic fly-wire
Plastic shopping bag
Large darning needle

step four Lay out sliver in a radiating pattern. If you want a design in the centre of the bed, put it on top of the layers of sliver (it will later be turned right side out).

step eleven The donut, lightly felted, as it should look before removing the template, and showing the extended tab cut open to allow for stuffing.

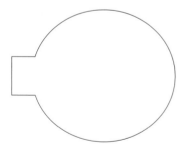

For the template, draw an oval, circle or square about 90 cm (36 in) in diameter (or a size to suit your pet; see page 77) on a piece of bubble wrap. Draw an extended tab to one side; this is the opening for stuffing the donut. If using a square, round off the corners slightly, as in the pictured examples. Cut around the outside of the drawing to make the template.

1 Make a template (see left). Lay the template on a bamboo blind and chalk an outline 10 cm (4 in) larger all around than the shape of the template. Take the template off the blind and set it aside.

2 Gently pulling off small amounts of sliver, begin to cover the chalked area, working from the centre outwards so the first layer of wool radiates like a sunburst. Lightly sprinkle the middle area (but *not* the outside 10 cm/4 in) with warm soapy water.

3 The next layer is laid out in an ever-increasing spiral, again working from the centre. Again, lightly sprinkle the middle area (but *not* the outside 10 cm/4 in) with warm soapy water.

4 Make one more layer in the radiating placement. If you wish to include a design on the donut, it should be laid out on top. Dampen the design as it is laid out, so that it won't slip. Repeat the wetting process and lay the template on top of the wool. Starting from the centre, carefully press down on the wrap (without bursting the bubbles), to smooth air bubbles out of the wool and evenly distribute the moisture.

5 Next, very carefully fold the extra wool at the edges in over the template, sprinkling it

step eleven continued Showing the template removed and the felt turned right side out. Apply soap through plastic fly-wire if necessary to secure the decoration.

step twelve Stitch the middle together, then stuff the donut with raw wool (as shown here) or your chosen stuffing.

lightly with water as you go. Ease and adjust in the corners where the tab extends from the main body of the template.

6 One side of the donut has now been laid out. Repeat the layers as before to fill in the area over the exposed template, extending the wool to the edge of the template.

7 When you are satisfied that there are no holes in the wool layers, sprinkle the entire parcel with warm soapy water. Lay a sheet of plastic fly-wire over the wool parcel, and gently pat the wool through the mesh, using your hands and starting from the centre. Once all of the wool has been wetted, you

can apply more pressure. A crumpled-up plastic shopping bag can also be used to massage the surface.

8 Keep gently massaging the surface, working carefully around the edges. Gently roll the wet wool pancake in the bamboo blind about 20 times. Unroll the blind and carefully turn the pancake over. Massage again using the hands and/or a crumpled-up plastic bag.

9 Repeat the processes, alternating gentle massage with gentle rolling in the bamboo blind, paying attention to the edges and making sure no holes appear. (If holes do

Calculating dimensions

For a custom-sized bed, first measure the diameter of the curled-up pet. Add 50 per cent to this figure; the total is how large the central (flat) part of the bed needs to be. Then allow an extra 45 cm (18 in) on each side (90 cm/36 in in total) to give a finished edge 30 cm (12 in) wide all round.

For a very large dog, it is best to felt several large flat pieces, sew them together, then stuff them, so you don't have to deal with a very heavy, wet parcel.

variation A mini version of the donut makes an unusual beading pincushion; the indentation in the centre can be used for holding beads or buttons as you sew.

mouse toy Components needed are a bundled wool core, tail, eyes and pre-felt for the body.

Hints

If you need to wash the pet bed, it is best to first remove all the stuffing and either wash it separately in hot water to destroy pests and their eggs, or to replace it with new stuffing.

The ping-pong ball and mouse toys can also be made around large seed pods, or using commercially available little belled toy balls as the insert.

appear, make small patches from pre-felt and tack them over the problem area using wool yarn. Then continue felting.)

10 When the felt becomes strong enough to pick up, the pancake may be picked up and gently dropped on the table a few times, to encourage the fibres to travel vertically through the forming cloth. This will make the donut stronger.

11 When the felt becomes smaller than the template, carefully cut open the end of the extended tab, sliding the template out. Turn the donut right way out, check the design is as you want it, and then roll it up on itself,

rolling back and forth from various directions until it is fully felted. Slide your hands in from time to time, to make sure front and back are not sticking together.

12 When the donut is felted satisfactorily, rinse thoroughly and dry. Then, taking a large darning needle and some woollen yarn, stitch an oval shape in the centre of the donut, stitching the front to the back in the process. This creates the little sleeping pad in the centre of the donut.

13 Stuff the outer ring with your chosen stuffing, then fold the tab ends inwards, and carefully stitch up the 'mouth'.

mouse toy continued Secure the eyes and ears with thread before completing the felting.

mouse toy continued Rub the toy gently with bubble wrap to felt the surface.

Mouse toy

First, scrunch a handful of scrap wool into a sausage shape and tie it up with yarn. Then felt pre-felt onto the surface of this shape. Add a tail (see page 17). To make ears, fold a small piece of sliver to make an ear shape, and wet the folded part with warm soapy water. Massage this area to make it firm. Pat the soft end bits into the body of the mouse, affixing them with some stitches if necessary. To make eyes, soft-felt two small button shapes from a contrasting coloured sliver. Tack to the toy at the partly felted stage using thread or wool yarn. Continue felting, using bubble wrap to protect the eyes until they bond with the rest of the toy. Alternatively, sew buttons on as eyes (but be aware that they may be chewed off). To continue felting, wrap the toy in bubble wrap, ensuring the ears are separated from the body by plastic as well. Hold the bundle together (not too tightly) with elastic bands and roll and pummel it about for 5 minutes or so. Remove the bubble wrap, and continue fulling using the fingers to rub areas that appear to need it. Gently rubbing the surface with a little scrunched-up bubble wrap will encourage faster felting. When done, rinse, dry, embroider whiskers if desired, then watch as your cat destroys your hard work.

Ping-pong ball toy

Lightly soap a ping-pong ball. Wrap in a few layers of sliver; spray to moisten. Take another piece of sliver 10 cm (4 in) long, dip all but one end in water and roll the wet part between the fingers to begin making a tail. Smooth the dry end over the ball and pat down gently with fingers. Spray with more water, soap the fingers slightly and pat and rub the surface gently to encourage felting. Remember to smooth the tail from time to time. When fully felted, rinse, pat dry and offer to your cat.

Alpaca bunny slippers

For a soothing, pleasant sensation, slip your bare feet into these soft shoes. The pair shown has an optional felted bunny for decoration. To make the slippers more durable, a piece of leather can be sewn to the soles.

This is an intermediate level project. When you are rubbing the surface of the slippers, the raw alpaca fibre will naturally spread out and become larger, so it is important always to rub towards the centre to keep the shoes the correct size. Once you feel that the felt is becoming a little harder, you can add more pressure.

To resize the slippers, measure the intended foot and add 16 per cent to account for shrinkage (as alpaca shrinks less than wool). This is the size to which the template needs to be cut.

Materials
White wool sliver
Alpaca fleece; if you buy raw alpaca fleece (that is, fleece as shorn from the animal's body, without being treated in any way) it must be carded (see page 9) before use

Tools
Washing board (optional)
Bubble wrap
Soap
Felting needle, if making the bunny ornament

Size
To fit 24–25 cm (9½–10 in) feet

step five Turn the parcel over, fold in the overlapping wool, then add more wool sliver over the area of the template, tucking in any fleece that is sticking out.

step six Fold the overlapping alpaca fleece (shown in brown) inwards.

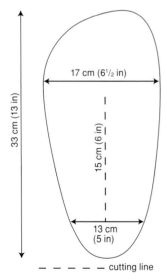

17 cm (6½ in)

33 cm (13 in)

15 cm (6 in)

13 cm (5 in)

— — — — cutting line

template The template will need to be flipped before making the second slipper, so that it becomes a mirror image of the first.

1 Cut bubble wrap to make the template (see Diagram 1).

2 Put one layer of wool sliver on the template, allowing 7 cm (2¾ in) overlap around the edges.

3 Put two layers of alpaca fleece on top of the wool sliver, each layer at right angles to the previous, allowing 7 cm (2¾ in) overlap around the edge of the template.

4 Sprinkle warm soapy water over all the fleece (taking care to avoid making it spread out due to water pressure) and press gently with soapy hands to make sure all the fibres are wet. Stroke the fleece very gently with the palm of your hand to create a flat surface, then massage gently only over the area of the template (not the overlapping wool) until soft felt forms.

5 Turn the whole thing over and fold the overlapping edges of the white wool sliver inwards. Making sure your hands are dry, add one layer of wool sliver, allowing 4 cm (1½ in) overlap. Sprinkle with warm soapy water and press gently by hand as in Step 4, tucking in any fleece that is sticking out.

6 Fold the overlapping edges of the aplaca fleece inwards. Add two layers of alpaca

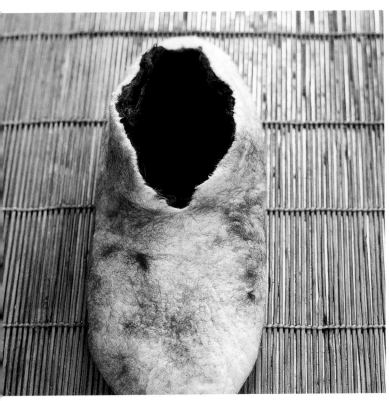

step ten Once the slipper has been properly felted, the two colours should have begun to merge.

fleece, each at right angles to the previous, allowing 4 cm (1½ in) overlap. Sprinkle with warm soapy water and press gently by hand as in Step 4, tucking in any fleece that is sticking out.

7 Felt for about 20 minutes on both sides, then squeeze 50 times in each direction.

8 Make a cut down the centre to allow for the foot to be inserted, then rub around the cut edges to felt them (put your hand inside the slipper and stroke hard, especially on the overlapping part). Turn inside out and felt as above for about 10 minutes.

9 Immerse alternately in hot and cold water and squeeze 50 times in each direction.

10 Scrub on a washing board (or on the ridged drainage surface of the kitchen sink) until the two different colours of fibre begin to meld. Stretch the opening a little to make sure it accommodates your foot. Allow to dry completely.

11 Make another slipper in the same way, firstly flipping the template so that the second slipper is a mirror image of the first.

12 When dry, attach a bunny to the top of each slipper, if desired (see right).

Felted bunny

The bunny is made using a needle-felting process, in which the wool is stabbed with a special needle that has rough, notched edges. These force the fibre down, making it entangle with other fibres and form felt. Using a needle to felt small areas gives precise control, so is ideal for areas of small detail such as the bunny's features.

Roll a ball of sliver between your palms until it hardens, then place it on a sponge, a piece of foam rubber or some other surface that you can stab into. Stab it with a felting needle for about 20 minutes, turning the ball to stab evenly all over, until it felts.

To make the nose and cheek, stab in little circles on the felted ball so that indentations form.

For the nose, roll a small amount of pink wool into a ball. Place in position on the larger felt ball and stab to fix it in place. For the eyes, do the same with orange wool.

For each ear, fold a piece of brown sliver in half widthways then place it on a sponge or other surface that you can stab into. Stab one end until it becomes hard, leaving the other end unstabbed. Position the ear on the larger felt ball and stab from the back, on the previously unstabbed end, to fix the ear to the head.

Baby blanket

This project is suitable for a beginner, and will

make a beautiful yet hard-wearing gift for a baby.

Use the finest Merino sliver for a soft, cosy rug.

Materials
White raw lambs' curls
Small amounts of yellow and pale pink wool sliver
White wool sliver

Tools
Bubble wrap or large bamboo mat
Soap
Towel

Size
Approximately 85 x 64 cm (33½ x 25¼ in)

step one Arrange the curly fleece in a spokelike pattern. Put a small circle of yellow sliver in the centre, then top it with a larger circle of pink sliver.

1 Cut a piece of bubble wrap about 77 x 105 cm (30 x 41 in), or mark an area this size on a bamboo mat. Arrange the lambs' curls in a spokelike fashion in the centre. Put a small circular patch of yellow sliver in the centre of the spoke pattern, then add a larger circle of pink sliver. Put two layers of white sliver on top, at right angles to each other, extending the sliver to the edges of the template.

2 Soft-felt the blanket, then hard-felt it for about 20 minutes. Stroke hard on the centre to flatten the pattern, then turn over and repeat.

3 Roll up the blanket and bubble wrap or mat together horizontally, then grasp and squeeze about 50 times. Immerse alternately in hot and cold water, grasping and squeezing as before, then unroll, re-roll vertically and repeat.

4 Put the felt on a work surface, pattern side up, and hard-felt it for about 10 minutes. Then roll it up vertically (minus the mat or bubble wrap) and grasp and squeeze from end to end about 50 times. Check the edges occasionally, firming them with the fingers to ensure they are crisp.

5 Do the pinch test (see page 39). When it passes the pinch test, roll it in a towel to remove excess water (do not wring it), then stretch the felt out in both directions to the finished size of approximately 85 x 64 cm (33½ x 25¼ in). Allow to dry flat in shade.

Variations

Other designs can be laid out in the centre of the template, such as flowers (see page 17), a bunny or, for a less traditional look, a geometric pattern.

Baby shoes

For these soft, pretty first shoes, use lambs'
curls and the finest Merino sliver to suit a baby's
delicate skin. Or vary the design by using wool
sliver alone, as shown in the variations pictured
on page 89. Once the baby has grown out of
them, the shoes will make a lovely keepsake.

For safety, if attaching beads or buttons to
the shoes, stitch them on very securely with
strong thread so that they will not easily
become detached.

Materials
Raw lambs' curls
Fine Merino sliver
Beads, buttons or embroidery thread (optional)

Tools
Bubble wrap
Soap
Scissors
Tissue paper

Size
Approximately 12 cm (4½ in) long

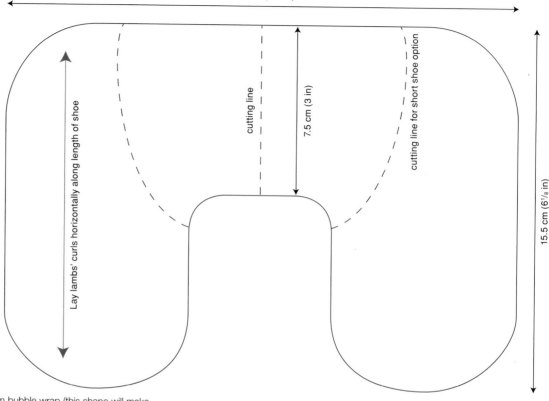

24.5 cm (9³/₄ in)

Lay lambs' curls horizontally along length of shoe

cutting line

7.5 cm (3 in)

cutting line for short shoe option

15.5 cm (6¹/₈ in)

template Cut the template from bubble wrap (this shape will make two shoes at once).

1 Cut out the template from bubble wrap. Note that you will be making both shoes at once; they will then be cut down the middle and separated.

2 Lay the lambs' curls horizontally on top of the template (no overlap is needed). Put two layers of wool sliver on top, allowing 4 cm (1½ in) overlap around the edges.

3 Sprinkle warm soapy water only on the wool covering the template (do not wet the overlap). Gently massage until soft felt forms.

4 Turn the whole parcel over. Lay lambs' curls horizontally on top of the template (no overlap is needed), then fold the overlapping edges of the Merino sliver inwards. Be careful that the wool is not piled up onto itself at the edges and that there are no lumps.

5 Put two layers of Merino sliver on top, with each layer at right angles to the previous. Sprinkle warm soapy water over the whole. Gently massage the wool until soft felt forms, tucking in any wool that is sticking out.

step two Lay the lambs' curls horizontally on top of the template.

embellishment The shoes can be decorated with stitching, beads, buttons, straps or animal faces (see 'Felted bunny', page 83), if desired.

6 Hard felt on both sides until the surface is smooth, about 10 minutes.

7 Cut down the centre of the felted piece, as indicated on the template, to separate the two shoes. Put your fingers inside each shoe and stroke the felt until smooth, paying particular attention to the corners.

8 Turn each shoe inside out and stroke the surface until it is hard and smooth, about 10 minutes.

9 Immerse in hot water and grasp and squeeze about 50 times in each direction,

then immerse in cold water and grasp and squeeze about 50 times in each direction.

10 Do the pinch test (see page 39); if you can grasp single fibres from the felt, it needs more massaging.

11 When it passes the pinch test, stuff each shoe with tissue paper and allow to dry in shade.

12 If desired, cut the top edge of each shoe to give a scalloped effect, as shown in the photograph on page 86. Embellish with beads, buttons or stitching (as shown in the photograph above) if you wish.

Glasses case

A soft felt case will ensure that your glasses don't get scratched or damaged. This easy project lends itself to personalized decoration, as shown in the pictured examples; lay down spots, or teardrop-shaped pieces of sliver to suggest raindrops, or add lines of hand-stitching, a crochet trim or a pattern of beads.

Materials
Wool sliver
Beads, buttons and yarns for stitched and
  crocheted embellishments (optional)

Tools
Bubble wrap
Soap
Scissors

Size
Approximately 20 x 9.5 cm (8 x 3¾ in)

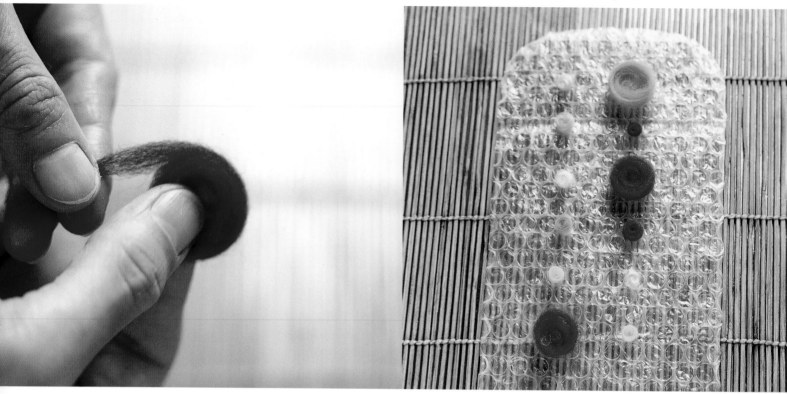

step two Decorate the felt by laying down a pattern before covering it with sliver. To create small dots, form thin lengths of sliver into spirals.

step two continued Begin to lay the pattern down on the bubble wrap.

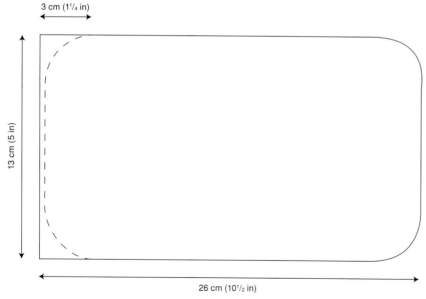

3 cm (1¼ in)

13 cm (5 in)

26 cm (10½ in)

template Round off the lower corners of the template. Once the pouch is felted and dry, cut the top of the pouch to form a curve, as indicated by the dotted line.

1 Cut bubble wrap to make a template.

2 Pull a little wool from the sliver and make a pattern, as desired. Lay it on the bubble wrap and gently sprinkle each layer of pattern with warm soapy water; this ensures the pattern won't slip and makes it easier to attach it to the background.

3 Put two layers of sliver in the background colour over the top, each layer at right angles to the other, allowing 4 cm (1½ in) overlap around the edges. Sprinkle warm soapy water only on the parts of the wool that cover the template (do not wet the overlap, and take care to avoid making the

step two continued Laying larger circles of sliver over small ones will create a two-toned dot on the surface of the felt.

finishing Crochet around the top edge of the case, or add beads or embroidery to embellish. As here, you can add a beaded loop to keep the pouch closed.

wool spread out due to water pressure). Gently press with soapy hands to make sure that all fibres are wet. Stroke the wool very gently with your palm to make the surface of the wool flat, then continue until soft felt forms.

4 Turn the whole thing over and fold the overlapping edges of the wool inwards.

5 Put two layers of sliver on top, allowing 4 cm (1½ in) overlap around the edges. Sprinkle with warm soapy water. Gently press with soapy hands to make sure that all the fibres are wet.

6 Gently massage until soft felt forms, tucking in any wool that is sticking out. Hard felt for about 15 minutes each side until the surface is smooth. Immerse the felt in hot water and grasp and squeeze about 50 times in each direction, then immerse in cold water and grasp and squeeze about 50 times more in each direction.

7 Do the pinch test (see page 39); if you can grasp single fibres from the felt, it needs more massage. When it passes the pinch test, cut the top of the case into a curve (as shown on the template). Allow to dry in shade, then add a button and button loop, and embellish if desired.

Wallet

This cute, sturdy little wallet acts as a mini handbag, with two pockets (one for banknotes, one for coins), a carry strap and even a photo pocket. To make a flower decoration, as on the example pictured here, see page 17.

Materials
Grey wool sliver
Small amounts of yellow and white sliver
   (or colours as desired), for the flower design
9 cm (3½ in) zipper, or size to suit your wallet
Embroidery threads (optional)
Bead(s) or button for closure

Tools
Bubble wrap
Soap
Sharp or crewel needle

step six Cut down the marked side to form two pockets, then turn right side out to expose the flower design.

photo pocket Attach the photo pocket to the inside of the wallet using blanket stitch. Leave the top edge open to allow for insertion of the photo.

1 Cut bubble wrap to make the template.

2 To make the flower pattern (see page 17), first put a yellow dot in the centre of one end of the template, then arrange petals around it. Sprinkle with warm soapy water.

3 Put two layers of grey sliver on top, at right angles to each other, allowing 4 cm (1½ in) overlap around the edges. Put a small amount of contrasting sliver on top of the pile to act as a marker, so that you know which is the design side when you later cut the wallet to form the two pockets. Gently stroke and massage until soft felt forms.

4 Turn the whole parcel over and fold the overlapping edges of wool inwards. Be careful that the wool is not piled on top of itself, especially at the corners. Put two layers of grey sliver on top, at right angles to each other. Massage until soft felt forms, tucking in any wool that is sticking out.

5 Hard-felt for about 15 minutes on each side until the surface is smooth. Immerse the felt in hot water and grasp and squeeze about 50 times in each direction, then immerse in cold water and grasp and squeeze about 50 times more in each direction. Do the pinch test (see page 39); massage more if needed.

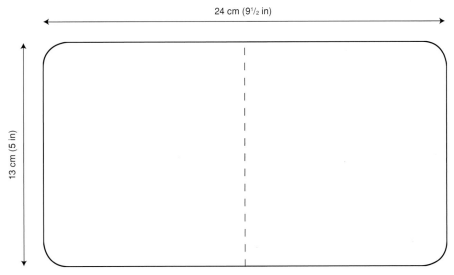

24 cm (9½ in)

13 cm (5 in)

template Cut a piece of bubble wrap to these dimensions for the template.

6 Cut widthways down the centre of the side that you marked with the contrasting sliver, as indicated on the template, using a pair of sharp scissors. Allow to dry in shade.

7 When completely dry, turn the wallet right side out, exposing the flower design, and insert a zipper into the cut that you made in Step 6.

HANDLE

1 Pull off pieces of sliver to give a length of about 60 cm (24 in). Form the sliver into a circle, making sure the ends overlap by about 8 cm (3¼ in). Dip the overlapping part into warm soapy water.

2 Roll the sliver between your palms so that the wool hardens and the circle ends up about 20 cm (8 in) in diameter. Allow to dry, then securely hand-stitch it to the underside of the wallet, along the fold line.

PHOTO POCKET

Make a piece of matching felt at least 11 x 11 cm (4½ x 4½ in). When dry, cut it to 10 x 9 cm (4 x 3½ in), or the same size as your wallet. In the centre, cut a window 7 x 7 cm (2¾ x 2¾ in), or a size to suit the intended photograph. Blanket-stitch the pocket to the inside of the wallet, matching the raw edges and leaving the top edge open. Finish as instructed at right.

Finishing

Sew a button loop to one end of the wallet (adding beads if desired, as on the pictured example) and a button or bead closure to the other end.

Mammoth tea cosy

This whimsical tea cosy will keep your teapot

warm and lift your spirits on a cold, wet day.

The cutting lines marked on the template are a

guide only; measure the teapot for which the

cosy is intended to customize it to your needs.

Materials
Raw fleece

Wool sliver

Small amount of contrast-coloured finished or
  commercial felt, for eyelashes

Wool or embroidery thread, for embellishment

Beads, for embellishment

Tools
Bubble wrap

Soap

Sharp or crewel needle

Notes
For the ears, you will first need to make a small
  amount of finished felt from grey curly fleece
  and grey sliver. Allow to dry, then use this
  from which to cut the ear pieces

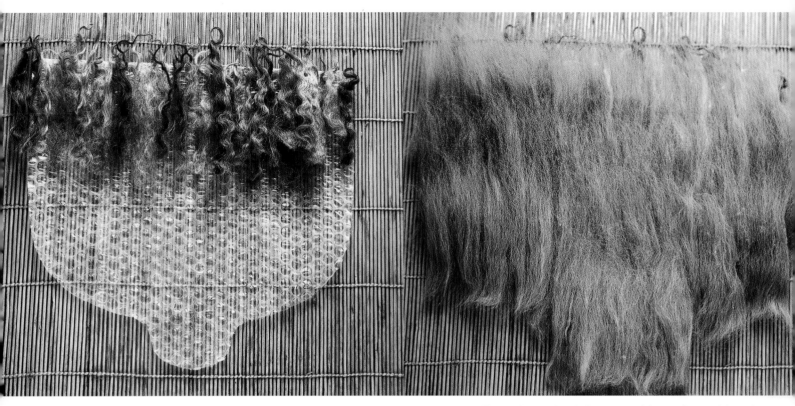

step one Lay strands of curly fleece along the straight edge of the template.

step two Put two layers of wool sliver on top of the template, at right angles to each other, allowing overlap at all edges except the straight edge.

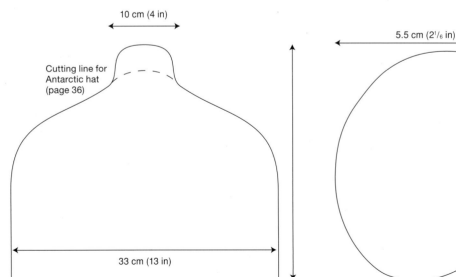

10 cm (4 in)

Cutting line for
Antarctic hat
(page 36)

33 cm (13 in)

template Cut a template from bubble wrap (this same template, minus the peak, is used for the Antarctic hat on page 36).

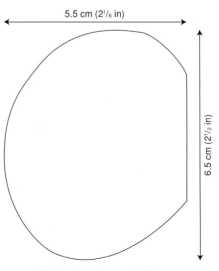

5.5 cm (2¹⁄₆ in)

6.5 cm (2¹⁄₂ in)

ears Cut two from grey curly felt

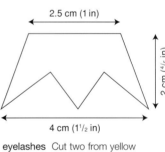

2.5 cm (1 in)

2 cm (⁴⁄₅ in)

4 cm (1¹⁄₂ in)

eyelashes Cut two from yellow finished or commercial felt

step five Measure and cut slits for the handle and spout.

finishing Sew a beaded loop to the top of the finished cosy so you can lift it easily off the pot.

1 Cut bubble wrap to make the template. Put one layer of curly wool on the lower edge of the template, allowing 3 cm (1¼ in) overlap at the edges.

2 Put two layers of wool sliver over the top, at right angles to each other, allowing 7 cm (2¾ in) overlap at all edges except the lower edge. Sprinkle with warm soapy water and massage only the wool covering the template (not the overlap) until soft felt forms.

3 Turn the whole thing over and repeat Step 2. Fold in the overlapping edges of the sliver then add two more layers, at right angles to each other, to cover the area of the template. Massage until soft felt forms, tucking in any wool that is sticking out.

4 Hard felt for about 15 minutes each side until the surface is smooth. Immerse the felt in hot water and grasp and squeeze about 50 times in each direction. Immerse in cold water and grasp and squeeze about 50 times in each direction. Turn the cosy inside out and felt for about 15 minutes, or until it passes the pinch test (see page 39).

5 Mark and cut the lines for the handle and spout. Allow the cosy to dry in shade, then add the mammoth's features and finish the cosy, as instructed at right.

Finishing

Add decorative rows of stitching around the top of the cosy, if desired. Turn up the bottom of the cosy to suit the height of your pot and stitch down in several places. Cut eyelashes from yellow felt. Cut two ear shapes from a 10 x 16 cm (4 x 6¼ in) piece of curly grey felt. When the cosy is dry, stitch the eyelashes and ears onto the front (the spout end) of the cosy. Add a small beaded loop to the top.

Beaded scarf

This unusual scarf is made of two narrow pieces of felt embellished with curly fleece and joined by two rows of beads. The larger beads shown here are made of felt (see pages 19–20), but you could use any type of bead.

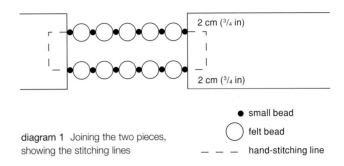

diagram 1 Joining the two pieces, showing the stitching lines

● small bead
◯ felt bead
– – – hand-stitching line

Materials
Curly wool
Wool sliver
Wool yarn
10 beads, about 2 cm (¾ in)
  in diameter
12 felt beads, about 8 mm
  (⅜ in) in diameter (see
  pages 19–20)

Tools
Bubble wrap, cut to 20 x
  100 cm (8 x 39½ in)
Soap
Scissors
Sharp or crewel needle

1 Arrange strands of curly wool horizontally along the bubble wrap. Top with two layers of wool sliver, at right angles to each other, to cover the area of the bubble wrap only (without any overlap). Sprinkle gently with warm soapy water (avoid making the wool spread out due to water pressure).

2 Press with your palms until the wool is thoroughly wet and any air bubbles have been pressed out. Stroke very gently (as though giving a baby its first bath) to make the surface of the felt flat. To make the edges round, massage them with your fingertips. When you feel the wool begin to harden, you can exert more pressure. Keep massaging for about 5 minutes.

3 Turn the felt over and remove the bubble wrap. Sprinkle with warm soapy water and keep massaging for about 5 minutes. If the curly wool isn't sticking to the felt, turn the scarf back over to the first side and keep massaging until it does (you won't need the bubble wrap for this step).

4 Immerse the felt in hot water and grasp and squeeze about 50 times in each direction, then immerse in cold water and grasp and squeeze about 50 times more in each direction.

5 Put the felt on a work surface and sprinkle with warm soapy water. Massage for about 10 minutes on each side, or until it is well fulled.

6 Cut across one end of the felt to give a clean line, then cut the piece of felt in halves lengthways. Allow to dry in shade.

7 Thread a sharp or crewel needle with wool yarn. Starting at a point about 2 cm (¾ in) in from the sides and 1 cm (⅜ in) in from the cut end, sew a line of running stitch (see Diagram 1), then string 6 large beads alternately with 5 smaller beads. Sew another line of running stitch at the cut end of the second piece of felt, then string the rest of the beads. Join to the first piece of felt and fasten off securely.

Bag with mobile-phone pouch

The body and pouch of this bag are felted

together, which is an advanced skill. A separate

rope of felt is used for the handle. However, if

your felting skills are less developed but you still

want to make a similar bag, you could make the

bag minus the pouch, and cut a patch pocket

out of a piece of matching pre-prepared,

completely fulled felt. Then, when the bag is fully

felted and completely dry, stitch the patch

pocket to the outside of the bag.

The white variation pictured has no pouch.

It uses raw fleece curls to form a fringe, and the

body and handle are felted together.

Materials
Wool sliver
Curly fleece (if making the white variation
   pictured at right)
Strong sewing or embroidery thread
Beads (optional)

Tools
Bubble wrap
Soap
Towel

handle For the handle, roll the wetted middle section of a long piece of sliver between your hands until well felted.

pouch Felt the lower section only, leaving the top part on both sides unfelted so that it can later be melded with the body of the bag.

HANDLES

Take two pieces of sliver, each 100 cm (39½ in) long. Wet the central section of one piece with hot soapy water and roll the wetted part in your palm for 20 minutes, leaving about 10 cm (4 in) unfelted at each end. Repeat the process with the other piece to make the second handle.

POUCH

1 Cut a piece of bubble wrap 15 x 9 cm (6 x 3½ in) for the template, rounding off the bottom corners. Put two layers of sliver on the template, at right angles to each other, allowing 3 cm (1¼ in) overlap at the edges. Sprinkle with warm soapy water.

Turn the whole thing over and fold the overlapping wool inwards.

2 Put two layers of sliver on the template, at right angles to each other (no overlap is needed). Felt the lower part of the pouch, leaving about 5 cm (2 in) at the top unfelted; this will be used to attach the pouch to the bag. Do not remove the template.

BAG

1 Cut a piece of bubble wrap 38 x 33 cm (15 x 13 in) for the template. Cut a horizontal slit in the template, about 9 cm (3½ in) long, and beginning 9 cm (3½ in) down from the top edge.

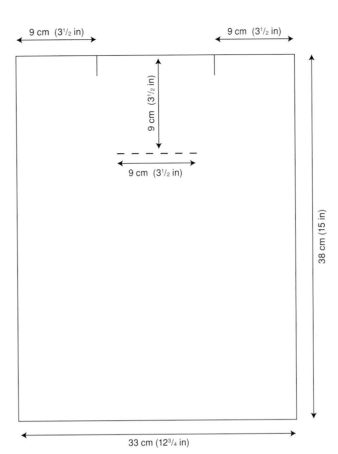

15 cm (6 in)

11 cm (4¼ in)

pouch template and mask Cut a piece of bubble wrap to these dimensions.

9 cm (3½ in)   9 cm (3½ in)

9 cm (3½ in)

9 cm (3½ in)

38 cm (15 in)

33 cm (12¾ in)

bag template Cut a piece of bubble wrap to these dimensions. The dotted line indicates where to make the slit to insert the pouch.

2 Insert the pouch into the slit cut in the bag template, leaving the bubble-wrap template in the pouch to act as a mask. Leave the unfelted top part of the pouch protruding through to the upper side of the template. Fold the wool at the back of the pouch upwards; fold the wool at the front of the pouch downwards (see photograph on page 108). This helps encourage the wool at the top of the pouch to meld with the rest of the sliver that you lay down for the body of the bag.

3 Put one layer of sliver on the template, allowing 7 cm (2¾ in) overlap at the edges. The unfelted top of the pouch should be above this layer. Then put another layer of sliver at right angles to the previous, allowing 7 cm (2¾ in) overlap at the edges. The unfelted top of the pouch should now be trapped between these two layers.

4 Sprinkle with warm soapy water, press the wool with your hand, fold the overlap inwards and massage until soft felt forms. Pay special attention to the entrance of the pouch, massaging more here to make a smooth connection with the body of the bag. Be careful that the position of the pouch doesn't move when you are stroking the piece, and that the pouch sticks to the body of the bag.

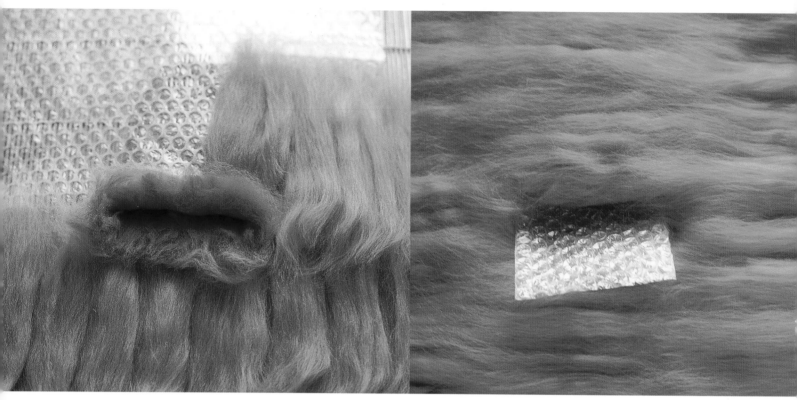

step two Insert the pouch into the slit in the bubble-wrap template, then lay out sliver to cover the template, allowing overlap at the sides.

step two continued Leave the bubble-wrap template in the pouch to act as a mask, so the insides do not felt together and the mouth of the pouch remains open

5 Turn the whole parcel over and fold the overlapping edges of wool inwards. Be careful that the wool is not piled on top of itself, especially at the corners. Put two layers of sliver on top, at right angles to each other. Massage until soft felt forms, tucking in any wool that is sticking out.

6 Immerse the felt in hot water and grasp and squeeze about 50 times in each direction, then immerse in cold water and grasp and squeeze about 50 times more in each direction.

7 Roll the felt in a towel to remove excess water (do not wring). Stretch the bag in both directions until it is flat and evenly shaped. Allow to dry in shade.

8 Attach the handles to the bag, placing them about 9 cm (3½ in) in from the sides of the bag and the same distance down from the top, making sure they are even. Stitch securely, adding beads if you like.

White curly fleece bag

1 Cut a bubble-wrap template 33 x 30 cm (13 x 12 in). There is no need to make a slit in the template for the pouch.

step four To attach the top of the pouch to the body of the bag, put your fingers inside the pouch and the other hand on top of the bag and massage well.

step five Once the first side of the bag is felted, turn the whole thing over and fold in the overlapping edges of wool, before adding two more layers of sliver.

2 Make the handles as described for the bag with pouch.

3 Lay the curly wool on the template, placing the cut ends about 10 cm (4 cm) from the bottom, allowing the curly ends to hang free over the edge of the template.

4 Put one layer of sliver on the template, allowing 7 cm (2¾ in) overlap at the edges. Put one handle piece at the top edge, positioning each end about 9 cm (3½ in) in from the sides. Put one layer of wool sliver on top, at right angles to the previous layer. Sprinkle with warm soapy water, press with your hand and fold the overlap inwards.

5 Felt the bag and handle together, being careful that the position of the handle does not move when you are stroking the piece.

6 Turn the whole thing over and repeat Step 3, then repeat Steps 4 and 5.

7 When the felt passes the pinch test (see page 39), allow the bag to dry in shade, then finish as instructed at right.

Finishing

When the bag is completely dry, sew a row of white beads 10 cm (4 in) from the bottom, along the line where the top of the curly fleece ends. Using backstitch and strong thread, stitch firmly, as this line will form the base of the bag.

Index

Published in 2007 by Murdoch Books Pty Limited
www.murdochbooks.com.au

Murdoch Books Australia
Pier 8/9, 23 Hickson Road, Millers Point NSW 2000
Phone: +61 (0) 2 8220 2000   Fax: +61 (0) 2 8220 2558

Murdoch Books UK Limited
Erico House, 6th Floor North, 93–99 Upper Richmond Road, Putney, London SW15 2TG
Phone: +44 (0) 20 8785 5995   Fax: +44 (0) 20 8785 5985

Chief Executive: Juliet Rogers
Publisher: Kay Scarlett

Concept: Tracy Loughlin
Art direction: Vivien Valk
Designer: Jacqueline Richards
Project manager and editor: Janine Flew
Photographer: Natasha Milne
Stylist: Sarah O'Brien
Production: Maiya Levitch
Project designers and makers: India Flint (Beads, Bowls on a ball, Stone door prop, Simple pod bag,
Honeycomb shawl, Shaggy rug with fleece curls, Champagne cooler, Soft cloche hat, Cobweb scarf,
Patchwork blanket, Reverse inlay rug, Origami bag, Donut pet bed and toy accessories);
Toyoko Sugiwaka (Antarctic hat, Kimono collar, Alpaca bunny slippers, Baby blanket, Baby shoes,
Glasses case, Wallet, Mammoth tea cosy, Beaded scarf, Bag with mobile-phone pouch)

National Library of Australia Cataloguing-in-Publication Data
Flint, India.
Felt : handmade style. Includes index.
ISBN 978 1 74045 882 5. ISBN 1 74045 882 6.
1. Felt. 2. Felt work. I. Sugiwaka, Toyoko. II. Title. (Series : Handmade style series). 677.63

The Publisher would like to thank Mel Koutchavalis
for her invaluable assistance in the production of this book.

Printed by 1010 Printing International Limited in 2007. PRINTED IN CHINA.